Buenos Aires

Buenos Aires

Original text:	Neil Schlecht
Updaters:	Nick Caistor and Ana Caistor-Arendar
Editor:	Douglas Stallings
Photography:	Neil Schlecht: 4, 11, 12, 15, 21, 23, 26, 28, 31, 34, 36, 40, 45, 46, 49, 50, 54, 55, 57, 58, 61, 62, 64, 66, 69, 71, 72, 74 (both photos), 79, 81, 84, 87, 88, 90, 91, and 93; Chris Coe: 3, 5 6, 8, 42–3, 77, 82, 96, 98, and 102
Cover Photograph:	Neil Schlecht
Photo Editor:	Naomi Zinn
Layout:	Media Content Marketing, Inc.
Cartography:	Raffaele Degennaro
Managing Editor:	Tony Halliday

Fifth Edition 1999 (Updated 2006)

CONTACTING THE EDITORS

Every effort has been made to provide accurate information in this publication, but changes are inevitable. The publisher cannot be responsible for any resulting loss, inconvenience or injury. We would appreciate it if readers would call our attention to any errors or outdated information by contacting Berlitz Publishing, PO Box 7910, London SE1 1WE, England. Fax: (44) 20 7403 0290; e-mail: berlitz@apaguide.co.uk; www.berlitzpublishing.com

CONTENTS

• A ☛ in the text denotes a highly recommended sight

Buenos Aires

BUENOS AIRES
AND THE PORTEÑOS

Buenos Aires. Listen to the way locals, the *porteños*, say it: *BwaynozEye*reys. The sound slides sonorously off the tongue. With the mere mention of their city's name, they sound as though they're about to launch into a tango. On the other hand, were they to attempt the unabridged name of the city – the noble title it was given upon its founding in 1536 – you'd think they were reciting an epic poem: Ciudad de la Santísima Trinidad y Puerto de Nuestra Señora la Virgen María de los Buenos Aires.

Saddled with that name, Buenos Aires might still be a hard-to-reach backwater with a few lonely Jesuit missions and some roughneck gauchos. But Buenos Aires today – just Buenos Aires, thank you – is the thoroughly modern capital of the world's eighth-largest country. More than a third of Argentina's 38 million people are concentrated in the Greater Buenos Aires sprawl. Yet this city along the Río de la Plata dominates the country in more than just population. It is Argentina's political, economic, and cultural epicenter, and porteños will tell you that their city is a world apart from the *provincias*.

But that doesn't necessarily mean that the rest of Argentina takes its cues from the capital. Porteños speak differently, with their own hyper-urban slang, and are more concerned – some would say obsessed – with appearing stylish and hip.

Buenos Aires, quite plainly, is a long way away from most places. It's farther from New York than Moscow is. Add to that Argentine legends of wide-open spaces, rugged gauchos, smoldering tangos, Nazi fugitives, and cuts of beef larger than the plates, and you've got a near-mythical place.

Buenos Aires's city center bustles just like any other modern metropolis.

The city, though, is no 'Wild South' theme park. It's a real, working metropolis, grappling with 21st-century challenges. It's an overcrowded city in an undercrowded country, a city where cellular phones and the Internet are being used more and more, but where the phone system only really began to work in the late 1990s. At the end of the 1980s, inflation threatened the country's entire foundation: growing at 5000 percent annually, there was a time when prices rose – literally – from the time you picked up a loaf of bread on the supermarket shelf to the time you got it to the checkout counter. For much of the 1990s, privatization was the rage. The phone company was privatized, the national airline was privatized, even the zoo was privatized.

In 1991 the Argentine peso was pegged to the US dollar resulting in lower inflation and higher investment. However, in late 2001, the country went into economic freefall. Bank accounts were frozen, unemployment sky-rocketed, and in one of the world's great food-producing nations, many people went hungry. Since 2003, the economy has started to grow again, and Argentines are once again optimistic about the future. But this is a country that rarely looks forward without also looking back.

At the turn of the 20th century, Argentina was a country of unexploited land and opportunity. Built upon massive immigration from Europe, it briefly became one of the richest countries in the world. Its capital, Buenos Aires – the last major city founded in Latin America – was called 'the Paris of the southern hemisphere.' The city's stately boulevards, classy cafés, and sophisticated, stylish inhabitants gave credence to the boastful moniker. For decades, Buenos Aires continued to be viewed – with both jealousy and disdain by other Latin Americans – as an anomaly in the region. A common aphorism says that the *porteño* is an Italian who speaks Spanish, acts French, and believes himself to be British.

It's a joke, but like all good jokes, it's based on some truth. During Argentina's 'Golden Age,' which began in the 1880s and lasted through World War I, the country sought and received millions of European immigrants. The government enticed foreign laborers, sometimes with far-fetched promises, to come and power the growing economy, populate the land, and make the country profitable. That they did. In 1910, when three-quarters of the inhabitants of Buenos Aires had been born in Europe, Argentines were recognized internationally for their tremendous agricultural wealth. Nearly half the immigrants came from Italy and a third from Spain, but workers and families also arrived from France, Russia, England, Germany, and Poland, as well as the Middle East, principally Armenia and Syria (President Carlos Menem's family immigrated from Syria). Immigrants built their Buenos Aires into a cosmopolitan capital.

Those poly-cultural foundations and sense of worldly confidence are still apparent today, even though the country experienced an unparalleled decline in the last part of the 20th century. What makes Buenos Aires so fascinating now, as opposed to its gleaming Golden Age, is that it is distinctly *of* the region, and not a misplaced, Europeanized island within it. Its European and first-world roots have blended with its Latino and indigenous character – and with its third-world difficulties.

Like Paris, Buenos Aires is a city of broad avenues, elegant apartment houses, sophisticated shopping streets, and bold monuments. Its Art Nouveau buildings are so European-looking that Budapest served as a stand-in for the city during the filming of the movie version of *Evita*. And Buenos Aires is cultured, there's no doubt about it. Its grand opera house is world-class. The city's café culture sparks impassioned discussions of art and politics. The nights are alive with theater and wee-hours dining. People have read and can recite their great writers: Julio Cortázar, Ernesto Sábato, and Jorge Luis Borges. Elegant couples in furs and hand-tailored suits attend the theater then sip espressos at corner cafés amid mahogany bars and tuxedoed waiters.

> *'It seems impossible that Buenos Aires once had a beginning: for me she is as eternal as water and air.'*
> – Jorge Luis Borges

Yet the city also exudes much of the culture and color of Latin America. Beyond the picture windows of the café, one of the old, colorfully decorated *colectivos* – public buses that wouldn't be out of place on the streets of Guatemala – rumbles by. The grandeur of the city's exuberant fin-de-siècle architecture is now somewhat decaying, in need of sprucing up certainly, but somehow it feels appropriate and real.

Buenos Aires's *barrios*, or neighborhoods, each have a noticeably distinct feel. Beyond the historic and official center of the city, visitors should make an effort to see how the old port area of La Boca differs in character from the elegant apartment houses and cafés of Retiro and Recoleta, or how the

Public artworks are a familiar sight in the streets of Buenos Aires.

wide-open green spaces of Palermo contrast with the colonial architecture and *conventillos* (tenements) of San Telmo.

Regeneration seems to be the urban theme of the moment in Buenos Aires. Old docks and warehouses situated along the river, and abandoned for decades, have been developed to become Puerto Madero, a fashionable area of restaurants, bars, and businesses. The popular new area has allowed Buenos Aires to reorient itself toward the port, from which it had long been effectively closed off. The empty arches under the train tracks in Palermo have been filled with restaurants and nightclubs. An old produce market has become the city's largest commercial center. Horse stables in Palermo Viejo have been transformed into an elegant indoor mall and restaurant area.

It's a new twist on an old theme; things are apparently new and better, but underneath it's mostly the same old Argentina. To the visitor who hasn't been to Buenos Aires for a while, the city looks good, and both the economic and political situation are improving. A major plus for tourists is that the devalued peso has made the country quite cheap to visit. It has also resulted in increased Argentine exports and foreign investment. That said, millions of Argentinians – around 20 million – are living below the poverty line, and those who can afford it have emigrated in their tens of thousands.

If you want to talk politics on your visit, you won't have much trouble engaging *porteños*, who are always quick to ask a visitor's opinion and to analyze their own city. Argentina had a torturous political history in the 20th century, with a litany of incessant unrest, repressive military rule, and the despicable 'dirty war' that resulted in around 30,000 people killed by paramilitary groups. That black era appears to be behind them now, but Argentines still love to blame the government and the miracle wealth that politicians seem able to create so effortlessly for themselves and their cronies.

A street artist in Recoleta.

As sophisticated as they are, *porteños* are also fanatics for their brand of pop culture and folklore. Several generations of *porteños* are rediscovering the nostalgic and melodramatic music of tango. They are also among the world's most impassioned fans of *fútbol* (soccer): the city is deadly silent when the beloved national team is playing an impor-

---

Lunfardo:
The Art of Speaking Like a Porteño

Porteños will tell you that their language is *castellano* – Castilian – but they have truly made Spanish their own. Indeed, the local Spanish may be unrecognizable at times to other Spanish speakers. Argentines speak a subsidiary language: *lunfardo*, a rich slang stew. *Porteños* are so steeped in slang that sometimes they can't seem to extricate themselves from their dependency on it. Ask the meaning of a word, and you may get a litany of slang in return. 'What's a *mina* (young girl)?' 'A *mina* is a *piba*.' 'What's a *piba*?' 'A *piba* is a *percanta*.' And so on. If you speak Spanish – but not Argentine Spanish – be prepared for some Abbott and Costello routines.

Argentine Spanish sounds quite a bit like South American Italian; many slang words are derived from the Italian of Genovese immigrants, as well as indigenous languages and Portuguese. Even the word for slang is slang. *Lunfardo* means 'thief'; and the language 'jail language.'

Certain words are identifiably, irrefutably Argentine. *Che* (pronounced 'chay') is affectionate Argentine for 'Hey you.' *Bárbaro* means not barbarous, but fantastic. A *Boludo* is a jerk. The prefix *re* is akin to the American 'way' (or, for non-Americans, 'very') added for emphasis (i.e., someone extremely old is *re-viejo*). And that is just the tip of the iceberg.

13

tant match, but it rockets into bedlam if Argentina wins. *Porteños* adore the simple, romantic notion of the *mate* ritual – drinking green tea – with friends and family, but they also plow into red meat and bottles of red wine like medieval hordes.

Buenos Aires is today a major business city, bringing managers and dealmakers in industry and technology here as never before. There are great tango clubs, old-world cafés, fine hotels, and Argentine *parrilla* restaurants serving that world-famous beef. For others with more time, a longer look at Buenos Aires will be rewarding. Trips to the River Delta, across the Río de la Plata to colonial towns and cities in Uruguay, and out to an *estancia* will give you a well-rounded picture of life in this part of South America.

No matter why you come or how long you stay, take a good look at the *porteños*. They're Europeans who are Latin Americans. They're fast-paced urban dwellers living close together in a land known for its lack of people and unending ranches. They are 'people of the port' without a proper port. They live in a city on a river that's not a river at all, but a giant basin – and even worse, the putative river is named for nonexistent silver. They are a people that were one of the world's richest and most literate just decades ago, but who are now struggling along with South American neighbors to compete on a global scale.

Is it any surprise, then, that *porteños* – residents of a city reputed to harbor more psychoanalysts than even New York and Vienna – are often said to be searching for some kind of national identity in this mass of contradictions?

If you're coming to Buenos Aires from the northern hemisphere, though, about the only serious contradiction you'll have to face is that it's winter at home but summer in Buenos Aires (or vice versa). And this is not a bad thing.

A BRIEF HISTORY

Discovery and Colonization

Buenos Aires and most of Argentina are so dominated by people of European descent that some visitors forget that Argentina was inhabited by native peoples, just as were the other territories in Latin America. Nomadic and warrior tribes stretched from northwest Argentina all the way to Patagonia and Tierra del Fuego.

Buenos Aires was the last major city in Latin America to be founded by European colonizers. Spaniards arrived first, in 1516, with a small expedition led by Juan Díaz de Solís. He named the body of water he saw *Mar Dulce* (Sweet Sea, later to be called Río de la Plata). The settlement didn't last long.

The Spanish explorer Pedro de Mendoza touched ground in 1536 and founded a small settlement – which many historians believe was near present-day Parque Lezama in San Telmo – but his expedition did not last either. Mendoza and his men encountered stiff resistance from hostile tribes, and they abandoned the outpost.

The first lasting foundation of Buenos Aires (technically the third, though most

Homage to the man who founded Buenos Aires, Pedro de Mendoza.

Historical Landmarks

1516   Spanish Juan Díaz Solís lands in region for first time.

1526   Sebastian Cabot names the 'river' the Río de la Plata.

1536   The Spaniards found the city.

1580   Juan de Garay founds the city for the second time.

1776   Spain elevates Buenos Aires to capital of Viceroyalty of Río de la Plata (today's Argentina, Uruguay, and Paraguay).

1806   English troops invade the city.

1810   On the heels of Napoleon's invasion of Spain, provisional government formed after sacking of viceroy.

1811–1820 Civil war between Federalists and Unitarists over provincial autonomy.

1816   Political independence formally declared.

1829   Juan Manuel Rosas becomes dictator and initiates repressive 23-year rule.

1852   Rosas overthrown.

1856   The First Constitution is drafted; the federalist system is imposed.

1862   Bartólome Mitre becomes first president of Argentine Republic.

1871   Yellow fever epidemic kills 13,000 people in Buenos Aires and pushes the city's aristocrats from San Telmo north to the neighborhood of Recoleta.

1880   Beginning of Buenos Aires's Golden Age of expansion and immigration.

1883   The first mayor, Torcuato de Alvear, initiates an urban plan of grand boulevards for the city.

1886   Buenos Aires named capital of Argentina.

1914   Debut of Carlos Gardel, tango singer.

1943	Military coup; Juan Perón is Minister of Labor.
1946	Perón assumes presidency.
1951	Perón reelected president.
1952	Evita Perón dies of cancer.
1955	Perón overthrown and forced into exile.
1973	Perón returns from exile and becomes president for third time.
1974	Perón dies in office; his vice-president and third wife, Isabelita, assumes presidency.
1976	Violent military coup intensifies harsh repression and censorship; Dirty War against putative subversives launched. Tens of thousands disappear over the next 7 years.
1980	Poet and activist Adolfo Pérez Esquivel wins Nobel Peace Prize.
1982	Military invades Falkland/Malvinas islands, prompting War of South Atlantic with Britain; Argentine defeat precipitates fall of military.
1983	Raúl Alfonsín of the Radical Party is elected president in a return to democracy.
1989	Carlos Menem, a Peronist, becomes president.
1991	Peso pegged to US dollar.
1995	Argentina becomes member of Mercosur, Southern Cone common market. Menem reelected.
1999	Left-wing Fernando de la Rúa becomes president.
2001	Economy collapses, resulting in rioting and currency devaluation. Government defaults on US$140 billion foreign debt.
2002	Eduardo Alberto Duhalde becomes president.
2003	Centre-left Néstor Carlos Kirchner becomes president. Return of steady economic growth and political stability.

Argentines consider it the second), was accomplished by Juan de Garay, a Spanish explorer who arrived in 1580 by way of Asunción, already a Spanish colony.

The colony was soon secured, and would be ruled wholly by Madrid through Lima, Peru, the early center of Spanish colonial administration. Yet, because of its distance from Lima and lack of a local labor supply, little importance was attached to the outpost. Its main purpose was strategic, to supply trade goods to Asunción and to interrupt the Portuguese contraband trade flowing in and out of Colonia del Sacramento (Uruguay). The Catholic Church played an important role in the new colony. Spanish Jesuits established an educational infrastructure in the city of Buenos Aires. In the late 17th century, prior to their expulsion by the king of Spain, the Jesuits made their mark on the city, building a number of halls and churches dedicated to education and the development of culture.

In 1776, the Viceroyalty of the Río de la Plata was created, and Buenos Aires became its capital. Toward the end of the 18th century, Buenos Aires grew in importance as a regional port and marketplace. The viceroy era gave impetus to a local fight for Argentine independence. British troops invaded in 1806 and 1807 as a reaction to the Napoleonic Wars in Europe, but locals succeeded in defeating the invaders, an episode in Argentine history referred to as the *Reconquista*. When Napoleon succeeded in deposing Spain's ruling dynasty, a provisional government in Argentina was formed on 25 May 1810, after the sacking of the viceroy – an event celebrated today as the May Revolution. In 1816, once again under threat of blockade and invasion, political independence was formally declared. The national and regional hero, José de San Martín, *El Libertador*, crossed the Andes and helped free Chile and Peru from Spanish rule.

Independence and the New Republic

The country, then known as the United Provinces of Río de la Plata, was soon gripped by the divisions between two congressional factions: Unitarians, who supported a strong central government, and Federalists, who advocated the autonomy of the provinces. The country fell under the long and cruel dictatorship of the *caudillo* (provincial strongman) Juan Manuel de Rosas (1829–1852). Rosas was elected governor of the province of Buenos Aires, but he was given (and then himself seized) extraordinary powers. During this period, the landed interests of the provinces took precedence over the port city of Buenos Aires. *Caudillos* from the interior, representing the large landowners, opposed centralized control of the republic. Rosas strengthened the country's conservative institutions – the military, the church, the mercantile and landed elites.

Rosas briefly stepped down but was reinstated in 1835 and given dictatorial powers. His oath of office pledged to inflict 'punishment and death to enemies of his government.' His regime adopted a militant political slogan: 'Federalism or Death.' The signs were clear, and the military, setting a precedent that would be repeated several times over the course of modern Argentine history, resorted to censorship, repression, and terror to stamp out supposedly subversive

You Call That a River?

The word *río* in Spanish may mean river, but the Río de la Plata (River Plate) – named by the explorer Sebastian Cabot – is not actually a river. It is an estuary, into which flow the Paraná and Uruguay rivers. Río de la Plata reaches a width of 200 km (125 miles), prompting porteños to call it 'the world's widest river,' but the basin is exceedingly shallow. It is also an unappealing muddy brown.

elements in Buenos Aires. Rosas governed exclusively by strongman tactics.

Foreign nations with mercantilistic interests in Argentina, especially Britain and France, tried to mobilize opposition to Rosas, and challenges to the regime included blockades of Buenos Aires. The Rosas government, after 23 years of repressive rule, finally succumbed to international pressures, both political and economic.

After decades of authoritarian rule, Argentines sought a form of representative government, and in 1853 they won a liberal constitution, the basis of which survives to this day, and a resulting federalist system. Bartolomé Mitre became the first constitutional president of the Argentine Republic. But the struggle between the port city and the interior continued. The system of federalism and tense relations between Buenos Aires and the provinces would take years to work themselves out. (In 1880, Buenos Aires was extracted from its province and made into a special federal district; La Plata became the province's official capital.)

> **An aphorism mocking Argentina's unique history in the Americas:**
> *Mexicans descended from the Aztecs.*
> *Peruvians descended from the Incas.*
> *Argentines descended from boats.'*

The collision between Buenos Aires and the interior of the country took on mythic proportions. While it was a political battle, it was also a fight for the soul of the country, the outcome of which would determine the authentic Argentine – the modern city dweller or the gaucho and *caudillo.*

President Domingo Faustino Sarmiento (1868–1874) spearheaded the cultural and political dogfight. Proclaiming his support of a modern, European, and constitutional Argentina, he led a fight of 'civilization against barbarism.' Sarmiento became famous for his tireless promotion of education.

The Golden Age

Buenos Aires led the drive toward modernity. The city possessed the port, and it alone was in a position to benefit from foreign labor, foreign ideas, foreign trade, and foreign capital. With the city of Buenos Aires as the seat of the national government, and Buenos Aires province losing power relative to the other provinces, the extreme tension between the city and the rest of the nation diminished.

Argentina embarked upon an era of spectacular growth, immigration, and political stability. The period between 1880 and 1910 is known as Argentina's

A visit to revered tango singer Carlos Gardel's grave.

'Golden Age.' Technological transformations were the engine behind advances in transportation, communications, and agriculture, and European immigrants provided the necessary manpower. The *criollo* (American-born Spaniards) and immigrant populations emerged with the political power to oppose the longstanding political might of the landed interior elites. Argentina's population doubled at the end of the 19th century, and it would double again by the time World War I had begun. The demographic explosion propelled the city's and the country's economic development, especially in terms of agriculture and crop cultivation. Argentina's educational system, supported by the new-found wealth, became one of the most distinguished in the world.

Though the country was still an oligarchy, political forces representing the masses of *criollos* and immigrant laborers were on the rise. Up to the end of World War I, Argentina achieved a consolidation of its political system and national economy. Based largely on livestock holdings, Argentina was on its way to becoming one of the world's wealthiest countries.

Argentina did not escape the Great Depression, as agriculture prices bottomed out and foreign investors fled. In 1930 the first military take-over of power in the 20th century took place, marking the start of a long, unfortunate tradition.

Argentina, Perón, and Evita

In 1946, a coup led by a nationalist military opposition ushered into power Juan Domingo Perón, a colonel who counted both the military and the workers as his great supporters. In 1946, Perón was elected president, and he would rule Argentina alongside his popular wife Eva (Evita) until 1955. Perón instituted a national welfare system and enacted a number of provisions designed to protect workers. The military grew suspicious of his labor alliances, however, and Perón's military support waned. However, his overtly nationalistic government continued to crush its opposition.

Perón's rule was ineluctably tied to the presence of his wife, Eva Duarte de Perón. Born poor, she resented and antagonized the elites, who never let her forget her humble origins. She was an important catalyst in drumming up popular support among the *descamisados* (working poor, literally 'shirtless ones') for her husband's regime.

Though Perón won reelection in 1951, economic difficulties and Evita's death from cancer in 1952 weakened his government. When it was rumored that Perón would distribute arms to the trade unions, the military struck, bombing the Presidential Palace and forcing Perón to flee the country.

Military Rule and Dirty War

The next 20 years were turbulent, as Argentina embarked on a violent program of 'de-Peronization.' His supporters were purged from every level of government, and even mentioning Perón's name in pubic was banned. The armed forces restricted political freedoms, but found it hard to govern in the face of opposition from Peronist loyalists and trade unions. Weak civilian governments also proved ineffective.

In the 1960s, the economy was on the verge of a breakdown, as was Argentine society. Worker strikes, student protests, and popular demonstrations were, although im-

Perhaps the most famous (or infamous) of Argentina's political personalities, Eva Perón.

passioned, routine. In the late 1960s in this once-rich country, one-third of all school-age children had no access to schooling. Factionalist guerrilla groups formed, and censorship of the media and arts intensified. The government passed laws against 'communism and subversion' and created a new judicial entity, the Federal Court Against Subversion.

In 1973 Perón emerged from hiding once again to assume the top post in Argentina's fragile political system. On his return to Buenos Aires from Madrid, two million supporters greeted him at the airport. A riot ensued; gunfire between security and demonstrators left hundreds dead and 1,000 injured. The economy was yet again in the midst of self-destruction. The powerful unions deserted Perón. His government became still more repressive until he died suddenly in July 1974. Greater chaos resulted – during which time Perón's third wife Isabelita tried in vain to rule – and was followed by one of Argentina's darkest periods.

General Jorge Videla and a military junta seized power – and, with it, authoritarian control of the government and the nation – in 1976. The military government launched an all-out battle against its opposition – both real and perceived – resorting to any means necessary to quash rebellion. Torture and terror replaced the rule of law. The abduction and 'disappearance' of students, journalists, activists, and political leftists became every-day occurrences. Argentina's unrepentant *Guerra Sucia* (Dirty War) was a war on its own people. As many as 30,000 people disappeared – most likely executed and buried in mass graves. Witnesses have testified to the paramilitary tactic of dropping the regime's 'opponents', alive, from military planes into the ocean. Many more dissidents emigrated, if they were lucky.

Despite international protest, a series of generals succeeded each other. However, the economy began to falter, and scandals arose. In 1980, the Banco de Intercambio Regional (BIR) failed, robbing 350,000 people of their life savings. Adolfo Pérez Esquivel, an Argentine human rights activist who spent a year under military detention, won the Nobel Peace Prize – a direct international repudiation of the military juntas.

But what finally felled their bloody dictatorship was the disastrous 1982 South Atlantic War (also called the Falklands War, or

> *'In any war, there are people who disappear.'*
> **– Argentine General Leopoldo Galtieri, July 1982**

Malvinas War, depending on whose claim to the depopulated islands off the coast of Argentina you support). The war was a weak attempt to defuse political and economic crises, and it failed miserably on both fronts. Argentina's swift defeat by Britain prompted new pressures for a return to democracy; General Galtieri resigned, and in 1983, a new hope, Raúl Alfonsín of the Radical Party, was sworn in as president.

New Democracy, New Beginnings

Alfonsín was initially a triumphant leader. The Madres de la Plaza de Mayo, the Mothers of the Disappeared, led Argentine society in demanding an accounting for Dirty War disappearances. In 1985, military generals and former heads of state Videla, Viola, and Galtieri received long jail sentences for their roles in encouraging crimes against the Argentine people. Alfonsín's government struggled until 1989; by then Argentina was in the midst of severe economic crisis, with inflation skyrocketing at around 5,000 percent annually.

In 1989, the Peronists returned to power under leader Carlos Menem. In 1991, Menem's government made the

A quiet afternoon in Buenos Aires: porteños *take a siesta in a Recoleta park.*

new Argentine peso equivalent to the US dollar – a move that proved extremely effective in combating inflation. Menem ruled in jet-setting, country-hopping style, amid allegations of corruption and nepotism. He was, however, re-elected in 1995.

At the end of President Menem's second term, the Radical Fernando de la Rúa was elected. He was forced to resign at the end of 2001, when the country went into economic freefall, and riots broke out. Argentina had three presidents in as many weeks. Parity with the US dollar was broken, and there was widespread economic chaos. In 2003, another Peronist, Néstor Kirchner, won the presidency. Since then, the economic situation has greatly improved, while political stability seems to have returned.

WHERE TO GO

Buenos Aires is a city of *barrios*, neighborhoods that have very distinct identities – *porteños* are defined by the neighborhoods they belong to. Although Buenos Aires has 47 different *barrios*, most visitors concentrate on the six or seven neighborhoods such as La Boca, San Telmo, Retiro, Recoleta, and Palermo. These, along with the center around Plaza de Mayo, hold the most history and attractions. A seventh neighborhood, Belgrano, also has much of interest but is a bit too far north for most short-stay visitors to Buenos Aires, and is not covered here.

Buenos Aires is flat, stretched out among the pampas plains along the estuary of the Río de la Plata. The city's major neighborhoods hug the banks (or at least the port), and proceed from south to north – following the

> Although the Argentine peso no longer has the same value as one US dollar, the 'dollar sign' ($) is used to denote pesos; 50 Argentine pesos is written as $50.

general development of the city. We'll begin, however, right in the middle.

MONTSERRAT AND EL CENTRO

Plaza de Mayo is the historical *corazón*, or heart, of Buenos Aires. The city was born here, founded by (or, more accurately, reborn under) Juan de Garay in 1580; the first foundation of the city actually took place 44 years earlier, near San Telmo, now a neighborhood to the south. But Pedro de Mendoza and his men established nothing of permanence, and the definitive founding is usually credited to de Garay.

Plaza de Mayo is a lovely square, with well-tended flower gardens, towering palm trees, historic buildings and, in spring, the lavender flower of the jacaranda trees. The square has been the site of virtually all of Buenos Aires's historic social and political episodes, from Evita's balcony pronouncements to her beloved workers to demonstrations in support of the Malvinas (Falklands) War and anti-military protests of the Madres de la Plaza de Mayo (Mothers of the Disappeared). Even today, all important political demonstrations convene here, and the square has held up to 40,000 people. Originally called the Plaza del Fuerte – for the city fort erected here – the plaza went through a succession of names, including Plaza de Armas, Plaza del Mercado, and Plaza de la Victoria, all reflecting the square's central importance and functions. It became the Plaza de Mayo in 1884 to commemorate the events of the May 1810 revolution that deposed the viceroy.

The grand Plaza de Mayo takes its name from the revolution that led to political independence.

In the center of the plaza is the 1811 **Pirámide de Mayo**, an obelisk crowned by the figure of a woman, honoring the revolution. Note the white handkerchiefs painted on the ground around the monument; they are the symbols of the Madres and their demands of the government to account for the Dirty War 'disappearances.' Their Thursday afternoon ritual appearances here in the 1980s were packed with emotion. The mothers and grandmothers of the disappeared no longer march, but they continue to put pressure on the politicians to uncover the truth about what happened to their loved ones.

On the west side of the plaza is the colonial **Cabildo de Buenos Aires**, the old town hall, construction of which began in 1725. Inside is a somewhat disappointing national historical museum with exhibits documenting Buenos Aires's history from colonial times. The changing of the guard here is an event rich with pageantry; uniformed regiments fire a salute upon hearing the '*Disparen!*' command on the last Tuesday of each month at 7.30pm.

Note the large **clock tower** near the *cabildo*. Until the end of Perón's reign, the clock marked the exact moment of Evita Perón's death, 8.25. The *cabildo* is flanked by the **Palacio Municipal**, the modern town hall.

Across Avenida Sáenz Peña is the **Catedral Metropolitana**, which stands on the site of the original church. Outside an eternal flame burns, for inside are the remains of José de San Martín, the national hero and liberator of the southern nations of South America. Construction on the church was begun in the early part of the 17th century, and it was christened the city's cathedral in 1622, but not finished until 1827. The long gestation period is reflected in the building's diverse architecture, from the austere neoclassical façade to the gilded Baroque altar, Italian-style naves, and beautiful Venetian mosaic floors.

To the right of the cathedral is the **Banco de la Nación** 👉
Argentina (Argentine National Bank), a 1939 Greco-Roman construction of marble and granite. The site has an impressive history: de Garay lived here; it was then occupied by a church, a cemetery, and later the original Teatro Colón. Designed by the renowned architect Alejandro Bustillo, the bank's lobby is an awesome expanse that might remind you of the Vatican, were it not for the unending lineup of bean counters' desks.

👉 At the east end of the Plaza de Mayo is the **Casa Rosada**, the palace of the President of the Argentine Republic. The reason for its pink color is a matter of debate, but it seems that pink was the only alternative to white in those days (and apparently no one wanted a Casa Blanca.) Note that the building, constructed in 1813, is asymmetrical; the original central Post Office, a separate building on the right, was joined to the presidential palace. The 'Pink House' is famous for its balcony, from which General Juan Perón and various other Argentinian leaders addressed their supporters. Beneath the palace is a tunnel, which Perón, under siege from would-be coup d'état leaders, used to escape in 1955. A small museum in the basement, open five days a week, features artifacts from Argentina's presidential history.

Directly across the Plaza de Mayo from the Casa Rosada 👉 is the wide **Avenida de Mayo**, which launched the modern layout of Buenos Aires. At the end of the 19th century, Torcuato de Alvear, the city's forward-looking first mayor, decided that Buenos Aires required the monumental architecture and grand geometry of Paris to claim its place as a New World capital. Avenida de Mayo, begun in 1889 and finished after the mayor's death, was the central axis in that plan. Its perfect alignment of important capital buildings recalls L'Enfant's layout of Washington, DC. The broad

*The President of the Argentine Republic works here, at the
lovely Casa Rosada.*

avenue links the presidential palace with the National Congress across town. Dignified Avenida de Mayo is reminiscent of Paris's Champs-Elysées. The tree-lined avenue is home to cafés, elegant iron lamp-posts, and handsome fin-de-siècle apartment buildings, all the same height.

Just beyond the annex of the Palacio Municipal (the old *La Prensa* newspaper building), you'll find the Estación de Subterraneo Perú, the first subway station in Buenos Aires and Latin America. Inaugurated in 1913, the creaky and cozy A-line cars you ride today on the 'Subte' are the original wooden versions.

Two blocks south of the Avenida de Mayo is the oldest collection of buildings in Buenos Aires, the so-called **Manzana de las Luces** (Block of Enlightenment). The square is bordered by Perú, Alsina, Moreno, and Bolívar streets. Spanish

Jesuits made their mark on the city in 1675, instituting a series of buildings and churches dedicated to education and culture, until their expulsion from Argentina in 1767 by the king of Spain. The first printing press was located here. On the enlightened block are: the German Baroque **Iglesia de San Ignacio**, built in 1713, making it the oldest church in Buenos Aires; the **Colegio de San Ignacio**, the former Jesuit school; underground tunnels built by the Jesuits; houses of the viceroys; and the former **Sala de Representantes de Buenos Aires** (House of Representatives, the old legislature building). Just two of the original five buildings belonging to the Jesuit Mission's **Procuraduría** (Administration), dating to 1730, remain. This site became the first University of Buenos Aires after independence.

It is only possible to visit the buildings by going on one of the weekend guided tours given by the Historical Research Institute of Manzana de las Luces, but if you can make it, the tour is highly recommended. It leads you into 18th-century tunnels, which are rife with folklore. Built for defensive purposes, they connected the viceroy's home and extended as far as the *cabildo* on the Plaza de Mayo. When the tunnels were discovered in 1912, investigators found weapons used against British invaders in 1806–1807, contraband liquor (evidence of how Buenos Aires became rich – contraband sneaked in the port), and evidence of torture and murder.

Just east, at the corner of Alsina and Defensa, is the **Basílica de San Francisco**, another of the city's oldest churches (1730); it's worth taking a look inside to see the **Capilla de San Roque**. Next to it is the old convent and Museo de San Roque, and across the street, the historic **Farmacia Estrella**. Still dispensing drugs today, the pharmacy has beautiful woodwork and allegorical ceiling paintings depicting health, sickness, and the wonders of medicine.

Next door, on Alsina, is the **Museo de la Ciudad**, a rather grandiose title for such a small place. The City Museum has quirky exhibits, such as a recent one dedicated to kitsch.

Museums and Other Attractions

Centro Cultural Recoleta. Junín 1930; tel: (11) 4803-1040; <www.centroculturalrecoleta.org>. Tues–Fri 2–9pm, Sat–Sun 10am–9pm.

Museo de Arte Hispanoamericano Isaac Fernández Blanco. Suipacha 1422; tel: (11) 4327-0272. Tues–Sun 2–7pm.

Museo de Arte Latinoamericano de Buenos Aires. Figueroa Alcorta 3415; tel: (11) 4808-6500. Wed noon–9pm, Thur–Mon noon–8pm.

Museo de Arte Moderno. Avenida San Juan 350; tel: (11) 4361-1121. Mon–Fri 10am–8pm, Sat–Sun 11am–8pm. Guided tours Tues, Wed, Fri, and Sun at 5pm.

Museo Nacional de Bellas Artes. Avenida Libertador 1473; tel: (11) 4803-0802; <www.mnba.org.ar>. Tues–Fri 12:30–7:30pm, Sat–Sun 9:30am–7:30pm.

Museo de Bellas Artes de La Boca. Pedro de Mendoza 1835; tel: (11) 4301-1080. Tues–Fri 10am–5pm, Sat 9am–noon and 2–6pm.

Museo del Cabildo. Bolívar 65 (Plaza de Mayo); tel: (11) 4334-1782. Tues–Fri 12:30–7pm, Sun 3–7pm.

Museo de la Casa Rosada. H. Yrigoyen 219 (Plaza de Mayo); tel: (11) 4344-3802; <www.museo.gov.ar>. Mon–Fri 10am–6pm, Sun 2–6pm.

Teatro Colón. Cerrito 618; tel: (11) 4378-7100; <www.teatrocolon.org.ar>; tel: (11) 4378-7132/3 for guided tours.

Teatro San Martín. Corrientes 1530; tel: (11) 4371-0111; <www.teatrosanmartin.com.ar>.

Teatro Nacional Cervantes. Libertad 815; tel: (11) 4815-8885; <www.teatrocervantes.gov.ar>.

The Obelisco, symbol of Buenos Aires, stands right in the middle of Avenida 9 de Julio.

At the corner of Defensa and Belgrano is the **Iglesia y Convento de Santo Domingo**, on the border of the Montserrat and San Telmo neighborhoods. In the front courtyard is the massive mausoleum of General Manuel Belgrano, a military hero to whom the creation of the Argentine flag is credited. The two-towered church, begun in the mid-18th century but not finished until a century later, was home to British troops during the invasions of 1806–7 (at the time, it had a single tower only). You can still see the damage caused by artillery fire; the **Museo de la Basílica del Rosario** inside displays the flags of the English invaders. Note the impressive organ, which is the finest in Buenos Aires.

Back on Avenida de Mayo, just a couple of blocks up Plaza de Mayo, is the symbol of Buenos Aires's café culture,

Café Tortoni. This evocative café, which dates to 1858, is Buenos Aires's oldest. Still a revered institution, it remains a thriving haunt of grand Art Nouveau décor, genteel service, hot political debate, and late-night nostalgia. Jazz and tango performances are scheduled, usually Thursday through Sunday, but you only need a coffee and a newspaper to pretend you're a newly arrived immigrant at the height of the city's grandest days.

Avenida 9 de Julio is, as any porteño will tell you, reputed to be the widest avenue in the world. Argentines must be taught this fact in grade school, because if you cross it five times in the presence of five different Argentine friends, you're likely to hear the mantra, 'widest avenue in the world,' for each crossing. Well, it is wide – some 13 lanes and 140 m (460 ft) across – and it looks impossible to cross on foot (you'll probably have to do it in stages). The avenue was built in 1936, exactly 400 years after the original Spanish settlement of Buenos Aires. To cut such a mighty stretch through the city, many 19th-century French-style mansions were razed. One of the few survivors is the French embassy, which defended itself with the claim that as a foreign entity, it occupied foreign territory.

Planted impressively in the middle of the wide avenue is the giant **Obelisco**, a dead ringer for the Washington Monument in Washington, DC, but nonetheless today a symbol and postcard image of Buenos Aires. It was constructed concurrently with Avenida 9 de Julio. Illuminated at night, the obelisk's central function seems to be as a rallying point for Argentine political demonstrations. If they don't end up in the Plaza de Mayo, they finish here.

Avenida de Mayo continues west all the way to the **Plaza del Congreso** (Congress Square) and the **Palacio del Congreso** (House of Congress). The plaza is a popular place for *porteños* to hang out and stroll. A fountain monument called **Monumento a los Dos Congresos** refers not to the two current houses of Congress, but those Congresses of the years 1810 and 1816, which were instrumental in the revolution and Argentina's independence, respectively. The Congress building, modeled on the US Capitol in Washington, DC, houses notable salons and an impressive library, the **Biblioteca del Congreso**.

Across from the Congress building are the new offices built for the members of Congress. There are often noisy demonstrations outside.

Avenida Corrientes is a central avenue, one that holds considerable cultural importance for residents of Buenos Aires. It

is lined with theaters, serious movie-houses, tiny bookstores, and cafés, many of them linked to the vocal intellectuals and leftists of yesteryear. One classic place that used to be drowned in smoke and loud talk, **Café de la Paz**, has been renovated; the makeover seems to have sapped the place of its special spirit. Corrientes is one of those streets that never seems to shut down, though parts of it seem a bit seedy late at night.

No, it's not a palace: the Aguas Argentinas holds offices – and water tanks.

The **Teatro San Martín** reflects the varied cultural interests of the area. With five stages and several exhibition spaces and cinema screens, it hosts dance, theater, and music performances, as well as film festivals, lectures and other events – something for just about everyone. **Centro Cultural San Martín**, with a competing agenda of cultural activities, is also found here, though its entrance is on Sarmiento. The **municipal tourism office** on the fifth floor, is a good place to get a map but little else. You're better off approaching the satellite tourist kiosks on Calle Florida.

While much of Buenos Aires is extremely attractive, the city's architecture is on the whole an eclectic mix, and many parts of the city are rather gray and drab, with attractive fin-de-siècle French-style buildings marred by a lack of upkeep and decades of traffic pollution. The neighborhood near Corrientes and Callao is one such area. While not necessarily dangerous, neither is it particularly pleasant for strolling. The carbon monoxide index in the city is consistently above the World Health Organization's acceptable maximum, a fact that you'll notice in this area.

In the area of Avenida Córdoba is an immense and spectacular building that seems a bit out of place in this congested area. The **Aguas Argentinas** building (national waterworks), occupying an entire block at Riobamba and Viamonte, houses both offices and massive water tanks. The audacious and eclectic building, which looks like an overgrown private mansion with a two-tiered roof, was designed in 1887 by the Swedish architect Karl Nystromer.

Back toward 9 de Julio, just west of the obelisk, is one of Buenos Aires's other famous landmarks, the **Teatro Colón**. The Colón was to have been completed in 1892, to mark the 400-year anniversary of the discovery of America, but was not actually finished until 1908. With a capacity of 3500, it has seven stories and took 18 years to build. One of the world's great performing arts showcases, its stage is dedicated to opera, symphonic music, and dance, and is especially noted for its excellent acoustics. Note the chandelier, inside which 10 to 15 people can stand and make sound effects. If you can't take in a performance, be sure to take the fascinating guided tour (in English: Mar–Dec daily 11am, 1pm, 3pm), which takes you right inside the theater, including its rehearsal rooms and set-building and costume workshops.

On the east side of 9 de Julio, just north of the Plaza de Mayo, is the **Microcentro**, the financial district, and the perfect grid-like streets that lead toward the Retiro neighborhood. Dozens of banks are located here. If you walk down Sarmiento toward the river, you'll run into the old **Correo Central**, the central post office built in 1928 by a Belgian architect. It is a spectacular example of French Beaux-Arts construction.

Just beyond the railroad tracks between the city and the river is **Puerto Madero**, one of the largest developments in Buenos Aires since the first half of the 20th century. The area was a harbor, or docklands, which held floating docks and warehouses and a series of linked dikes. The long-abandoned warehouses have now been carefully converted, preserving the wood-and-iron buildings into spaces that house restaurants, bars, car dealerships, and a few residential lofts.

The restoration of some 20 warehouses began in 1990, and the area quickly became very popular and quite chic; many fashionable restaurants in Recoleta and the Costanera Norte moved here and brought their clients with them. The restaurants are particularly crowded at mid-day, when bankers and government employees walk over for lunch. There are many spectacular new hotels, and the Torres El Faro, Buenos Aires' tallest building at 170 m (560 ft) high.

The Anfiteatro Puerto Madero hosts musical events, film shows, and festivals.

Behind the remainder of the docks that are undergoing renovation is an ecological reserve called the **Parque Natural y Reserva Ecológica Costanera Sur**. Despite its grandiose name, it's a wild area of some 500 sq km (190 sq miles) that is home to a variety of plant and wildlife and abuts the Río de la Plata. *Porteños* come here to run and cycle, but for the tourist there's not much to see, unless you're in the mood for exercise.

If you look back toward the Casa Rosada, you'll see a monumental sculpture of **Colón** (Columbus), a gift from Italy.

The Old and New Abasto

In the spirit of the *reciclaje* (recycling) fever that gripped Buenos Aires in the late 20th century, a famous produce market in one of the city's worst neighborhoods became one of its largest shopping centers. The giant Abasto market on Corrientes near Agüero was abandoned over 20 years ago and was reborn as a shopping mall in 1999. The 12,000-sq-m (130,000-sq ft), 5-story mall contains more than just shops: its restaurants, cinemas, theaters, children's museum, supermarket, and hotel make it an important focus for the local community.

The Abasto mall truly stands out in the surrounding neighborhood, and not just because of the fantastic illumination it receives at night. The legendary tango singer Carlos Gardel hailed from this *barrio* and the mall is themed around him. Once one of Buenos Aires's seedier zones, full of crumbling and abandoned buildings, the area has enjoyed something of a renaissance, symbolized by the mall dedicated to the 'kid from Abasto', and property values have shot up.

Birthplace of the tango, La Boca offers local color and a good deal of history as well.

LA BOCA

If Plaza de Mayo is the heart of the city, La Boca, to the south, may be its soul. The port area at the mouth *(boca)* of the Riachuelo Canal is one of the oldest residential neighborhoods in Buenos Aires. In the mid-19th century, Argentina faced a population crisis. It appealed for immigrants, who came in two great waves: one in 1870 and another in the 1930s. Italian immigrants, a great many of them Genovese, working in the shipyard as sailors and longshoremen largely populated La Boca. They were contracted laborers who arrived to find little infrastructure awaiting them; they built their simple houses from the materials that went into shipbuilding – mainly wood, cement, and tin – sometimes filling them with as many as 15 families.

La Boca is said to be the birthplace of the tango, inspired by the marginalized community of men who frequented the port's brothels. Tango was the product of late 19th-century working-class, immigrant neighborhoods; the music, at once nostalgic and realistic, was, perhaps, the Argentine equivalent of the American blues.

Although the working-class neighborhood is finally making something of a comeback, the main reason it is known to tourists is for **El Caminito**, the brilliantly painted little alleyway that was conceived by one of the *barrio's* most famous sons. Local artist Benito Quinquela Martín (1890–1977) transformed the street to give the working population something to be proud of, and local artists a place to display their talents. Deeply influenced by the vibrant neighbourhood in which he grew up, Quinquela was a proponent of strong emotional colors in his paintings. Some say that the residents of La Boca were too poor to buy paint, and they used whatever they could pick up from the shipyard, meaning that they would have to cobble together several colors from leftover supplies to paint their houses.

El Caminito, which means simply 'little path,' is just one block long and begins at **La Vuelta de Rocha**, facing the Riachuelo. The street's walls are filled with bas-relief sculptures and murals, many of them inspired by the tango. The simple houses are painted vibrant blue, yellow, orange, red, and green, and, as in Naples, they usually have laundry strung outside. One house at the end of El Caminito is a painted puzzle made from the colors of the Argentine, Italian, and Spanish flags. On weekends and most days during the spring and summer, you can find local artists hawking their artwork, just as Quinquela intended. As many observers have pointed out, La Boca is literally Buenos Aires's most colorful neighborhood.

Most tourists do a quick run-through of El Caminito, snap some photos, perhaps buy a souvenir picture from one of the local artists, and head on to another neighborhood. You'll need a little more time if you wish to connect the colorful street with the roots of La Boca, which are also in large part the roots of Buenos Aires.

At the end of El Caminito, and off to the left past the railroad tracks, are examples of period houses that have not been spruced up with bright paint. Here you'll get a real feel for the structure and materials used in La Boca houses; note the separate staircases on some, used as private entryways for the families sharing living quarters. A train, long defunct, once ran from La Boca all the way to Retiro. Private interests are seeking to raise funds to reinstitute the train; it would be a superb vehicle for visitors to the city, as well as residents.

The **Museo de Bellas Artes de La Boca**, back on the main street Pedro de Mendoza, near La Vuelta de Rocha, may not seem like much at first. But its place in the neighborhood is important. The museum is the former studio and living quarters of Quinquela Martín. He painted what he saw living in the port *barrio*: men working on ships, great fires engulfing the port, and the years of decay, when the port lay polluted and dormant, its ships like the carcasses of monsters. Quinquela became a rather important painter in Argentina; a story oft-told is that the Italian dictator Benito Mussolini offered to buy one of his paintings with a blank check, and that Quinquela refused. That painting hangs in the museum. Look also for the 19th-century ship figureheads, several deteriorated from their many years at sea.

The museum looks out onto the port, which remains as it was in Quinquela's last days: a ship's graveyard, not an example of living history, but of neglect and decadence. Many of the ships are half sunk, and the Riachuelo is said to be so polluted that no living organism remains. When you near the smelly port, you'll feel far removed from a city named 'Good Airs.'

In addition to El Caminito, La Boca has another claim to fame. The *barrio* is

This mural depicting immigrant dockers is one of many on El Caminito.

in the shadows of the famous **La Bombonera** football (soccer) stadium, where Argentina's most beloved team, the Boca Juniors, play. Diego Maradona, the controversial footballer who led Argentina to World Cup victory in 1986 with his 'hand of God' goal, made his mark here. A series of mosaic murals near the stadium depicts, in the colors of Boca Juniors, the neighborhood's central themes: immigrants, tango, and *fútbol*.

Long a marginal neighborhood, in the late 1990s La Boca began to draw a small influx of new residents and artists, who are buying and fixing up some traditional homes. Several of the simple, Italian-style houses around the Vuelta de la Rocha are newly renovated, and a flashy new art gallery, the PROA **Foundation**, has established a space in the large white house on Pedro de Mendoza.

La Boca is a long way from becoming gentrified, though. Beyond the Avellaneda Bridge is a street called **Calle Necochea**, lined with decadent Italian cantinas, dance halls, and inexpensive restaurants. In its heyday, sailors and port residents looking for love used to whoop it up here. Some of the cantinas are rather dilapidated, but they are pretty harmless. A tired sidewalk hawker may call out 'have a look!' and you can, but it's not a good area to be wandering around alone with camera in hand. Many of the sleazier brothels that inspired the tango are on this street or near here, and the neighborhood isn't much more respectable now than it was then.

SAN TELMO

The tango was born in La Boca, but its spirit really lives on in the bohemian *barrio* of San Telmo. The neighborhood immediately to the north of La Boca is a charming mass of antiques stores, *conventillos* (former immigrant tenements), timeless cafés and restaurants, and grand, slightly shabby houses that wouldn't look out of place in Havana. It is a neighborhood that wears its artistic and intellectual character on its sleeve, whether during the day in cafés or in the wee hours at tango clubs and rowdy bars.

This historic *barrio*, an urban nucleus since the 17th century, is about as porteño as the city has to offer. It has been inhabited by slaves, rich landowners, and European entrepreneurs. Many of Buenos Aires's grand families lived here in colonial times, before the yellow fever of 1871 had them escaping to higher ground in the northern neighborhoods of

Some locals are ready for a traffic-stopping tango anytime and anywhere.

Retiro and Recoleta. After the epidemic, which wiped out more than 13,000 people, waves of Italian and Spanish immigrants arrived. They converted the mansions into multifamily *conventillos*; through the mid-20th century, San Telmo acquired a rather unsightly and unseemly character.

These same houses have undergone a third incarnation: today they hold restaurants, antiques shops, and artists' studios, and the neighborhood has been revived. The predominant style of architecture, famous in Buenos Aires, is the *casa de chorizo* – 'sausage house,' or rowhouse, so called for

Antique **mates** *embellished with silver are a souvenir particular to Buenos Aires.*

its squatty, narrow, linked nature. *Casas de chorizo* always encase a central patio.

The area draws multitudes to its renowned **Feria de San Telmo** (Sunday antiques fair) at the Plaza Dorrego, the heart of the neighborhood. During the week, the square holds tables for the bars and restaurants that line it, but by 10am Sunday, the plaza is filled with booths selling antique *mates*, silver, books, phonographs, and medicine bottles, among many other items. It is part flea market and part serious antiques market. If your interest is piqued but you don't find exactly what you're looking for, there are many antiques shops, some of them exquisite, on the neighboring streets – particularly along Calle Defensa. The *feria* always features tourist-oriented tango dancing, both in the surrounding streets and in the plaza as the market begins to taper off.

A half block from Plaza Dorrego is the **Iglesia Nuestra Señora de Belén**, also known as the Iglesia de San Telmo. The church, with a Baroque façade, was begun by the Jesuits in the mid-18th century, but construction consumed seven decades. Students from the Facultad de Medicina (Medical College) once performed dissections on cadavers in the small chapel next to the sacristy.

San Telmo is an excellent neighborhood for strolling during the day. Walk along Balcarce, Estados Unidos streets, and cobblestoned Pasaje de San Lorenzo. If you get the chance, peek in one of the lovely old homes to catch a glimpse of its central patios. A good place to do this without violating anyone's privacy is the **Pasaje de la Defensa** house, on Calle Defensa at San Juan. It's a magnificent example of a 19th-century *casa de chorizo*, with a large central patio and balconies. Built in 1880, the residence demonstrates that San Telmo *barrio* didn't fall into complete decay after the yellow fever outbreak. The black-and-white marble floors are original. It now houses a handful of hand-craft and antiques shops and a bar in the back, up the stairs.

On Avenida San Juan, 350 is the **Museo de Arte Moderno**, a large, old red-brick warehouse, once a cigarette factory. The museum has a scant permanent collection, but puts on many touring shows of interest.

A relatively new addition, on Piedras 720, is the **Museo Vivo del Tango**, a small and rather commercial venture.

A bit farther south is sloped **Parque Lezama**, which has its entrance on Brasil and Defensa. The entrance is marked by an imposing statue of Don Pedro Mendoza, the original settler of Buenos Aires, in full conquistador regalia (many believe this to be the exact site of the city's founding). Once one of Buenos Aires's most beautiful spots, Lezama park

---

Crowded House

Someone who speaks loudly is sometimes called a *conventillero* — slang that owes its existence to the Italian immigrants who shared the tenements called *conventillos* with other families, and had to yell to be heard over the din of all those housemates.

---

today is barely covered with grass. Nevertheless, it's a decent enough spot to relax while visiting San Telmo.

Within the park but entered from Calle Defensa is the terracotta-colored **Museo Histórico Nacional** (National History Museum). Across from the museum is a block of lovely French-style buildings.

On the other side of the park, on Avenida Brasil, is the late 19th-century **Russian Orthodox Catholic Church** – whose five bright blue Byzantine cupolas certainly stand out on the Buenos Aires skyline.

At night San Telmo pulses, mostly with the melancholic chords of the *bandoneón*, the distinctive accordion-like instrument of the tango. All over the *barrio*, there are nightly tango performances, some more touristy than others, at small late-night clubs on quiet streets. Tango clubs include intimate Bar Sur, the ever-popular El Viejo Almacén, Casa Blanca and Michelangelo. For additional information on going out at night in San Telmo, *see page 82*. Even if you're not planning to view a tango performance (you are in Buenos Aires, though), the unique character of San Telmo is quite apparent at night; it's a good place for dinner and bar-hopping.

The eastern border of San Telmo is Paseo Colón, where you can catch a bus or taxi for one of the northern neighbor-

If She'd Done It Her Way

Evita Perón had herself hoped to be buried in Plaza Olazábal in San Telmo, in a crystal coffin within a monument three times the size of the Statue of Liberty. Those grandiose plans had to be scuttled, however. The political opponents who stole her corpse and whisked it furtively out of Argentina – it remained in Europe for almost 20 years – ensured that there would be no such monument. Evita now lies, of course, in Recoleta Cemetery (see page 55).

Tango, tango everywhere – this huge mural depicting the torrid dance is in San Telmo.

hoods. Before you leave San Telmo behind, make a point of seeing the immense **mural** depicting tango at the corner of Independencia and Balcarce, as well as the well-executed sculpture *Canto al Trabajo*, by the Argentine artist Rogelio Yrurtia, in the middle of Plaza Olazábal.

Across the avenue is the authoritarian **Facultad de Ingeniería** (Engineering Faculty), which looks as though it may have been commissioned by Mussolini. One block behind it is the Confederación General de Trabajo (CGT, or General Confederation of Labor, the Peronist workers' union) building, which displays a small mosaic and eternal flame dedicated to the workers' hero, Evita.

RETIRO AND BARRIO NORTE

Retiro is an elegant northern neighborhood where Buenos Aires's European heritage really shines. The centerpieces of the *barrio* are Plaza San Martín and the Retiro train station. It is also an area of pedestrian shopping streets, art galleries, hotels, restaurants, and cafés. The grid-like commercial area around Calle Florida straddles the centro and Retiro, and can as easily be seen when visiting Plaza San Martín as when seeing the Plaza de Mayo.

Historic **Plaza San Martín** is one of the city's most precious green spaces, a lovely respite from downtown where mothers and small children, lovers, and businessmen come to walk under the enormous palms and sit beneath the *palos borrachos* trees. The plaza is particularly appealing in spring, when the purple jacaranda trees bloom around its fringes.

Plaza San Martín itself was once the site of slave trading, battles with English invaders, a bullring, and the city's Museum of Fine Arts. The monuments and handsome early 20th-

Plaza San Martín is an oasis of green surrounded by the hustle and bustle of downtown Buenos Aires.

century buildings that ring the plaza attest to its historical importance. The Art-Nouveau **Palacio San Martín** now belongs to the Ministry of Foreign Service. **Círculo Militar**, which houses a Weapons Museum, was once the Palacio Paz, the largest private residence in Argentina in 1890. The building at the corner of Calle Florida is a former private mansion that now belongs to **Parques Nacionales**.

Down the hill from the plaza – the slope marks the point to which the Río de la Plata once rose – is the 1916 **Torre Monumental**, a Big Ben imitator – once known as Torre de los Ingleses as it was a present from the English in 1910 to celebrate the centenary of the Argentine Revolution. Recently renovated, there are now guided tours of the tower. Also here is the **Monumento a los Héroes de la Guerra de las Malvinas**, which documents the names of the Argentine troops killed in the 1982 war.

Estación de Retiro, the city's principal train station, is just across Avenida Mejía from the Torre Monumental. Built in 1908, it was one of the largest train stations in the world at the time. This is where visitors who wish to go to Tigre and the River Delta north of Buenos Aires catch the train.

The block bordered by Corrientes, Suipacha, Marcelo T. Alvear, and San Martín, just south of Plaza San Martín, is an important commercial area. These streets once displayed some of Buenos Aires's finest buildings. While many have fallen victim to the city's 20th-century expansion, there are still some handsome examples of Belle-Epoque architecture. A couple of the streets are pedestrian-only and emblematic of Buenos Aires's proud heritage. **Lavalle** is lined with movie theaters, cafés, and restaurants, while **Calle Florida** has long been famous as Buenos Aires's central shopping promenade. Look for the Banco de Boston and its massive imported stone entranceway. On a leisurely stroll, several tea-rooms (such as the Hotel Richmond), leather shops, and bookstores (including the large and inviting El Ateneo, which stocks English-language titles) compete for your attention. Sadly, since the 2001 riots, Calle Florida, once an elegant and refined open-air mall, has become somewhat down-at-heel: a jumbled mass of electronics and jeans shops for the *masas*.

The elite, though, still have **Galerías Pacífico**, a strikingly ornate shopping center at the corner of Florida and Córdoba. It must be one of the few shopping centers to be declared a national historical monument. Envisioned at the end of the 19th century as the 'Bon Marché Argentino,' it occupies an entire city block and took much of the 20th century to complete. The gallery features a central cupola with neo-realistic murals, executed in the mid-1940s by five Argentine painters. Within the shopping center is the **Centro Cultural Borges**, featuring a variety of dance, music, and art exhibits.

North of Plaza San Martín (at Suipacha, 1422), is an attractive, small museum: **Museo de Arte Hispanoamericano Isaac Fernández Blanco**. This small collection of 16th–19th-century colonial and Latin American art and artifacts is one of the most important of its kind in South America. It's housed in the magnificent neocolonial Noel Palace, which was constructed in 1920. Fernández Blanco built a remarkable collection of silver from Alto Peru and Río de la Plata, paintings from the Alto Peru and Cuzco, objects from Jesuit missions, polychrome figures from Quito, and Luso-Brazilian furniture and decorative arts. The splendid Spanish-style gardens are an ideal place to relax.

Just west of Avenida 9 de Julio, at Avenida Alvear, is the historic **Embajada de Francia** (French embassy), which resisted demolition. The lengthy, curved **Avenida Santa Fé**, one of Buenos Aires's most prestigious addresses, begins at Plaza San

Primary Buenos Aires Attractions

Plaza de Mayo. The historical heart of Buenos Aires; the site of all important political demonstrations.

Avenida de Mayo. Buenos Aires's grand boulevard, linking the presidential palace with the national congress.

Manzana de las Luces. This 'Block of Enlightenment' is lined with the oldest surviving collection of buildings in Buenos Aires.

Café Tortoni. Historic café; a place for lively political debate, tango performances, or simply a cup of coffee.

Obelisco and Avenida 9 de Julio. The widest avenue in the world, as any porteño will tell you; the obelisk, located in its center, is a popular postcard image of Buenos Aires.

Teatro Colón. This historic theater is one of the world's great performing arts spaces.

Puerto Madero. A former warehouse district that has become the spot for fashionable restaurants and bars.

La Boca's El Caminito. Short block of brilliantly painted houses; Buenos Aires's most colorful neighborhood.

Feria de San Telmo. Every Sunday at 10am the Plaza Dorrego in San Telmo plays host to this antiques fair.

Plaza San Martín. This lovely park is one of the centerpieces of Retiro.

Cementerio de La Recoleta. The place where Argentina's notables are buried, including Eva Perón.

Museo Nacional de Bellas Artes. The largest and most important art museum in Argentina, housing works by European masters such as Tintoretto, El Greco, and Renoir.

Palermo Chico. This area of historic French-style homes in Palermo is the location of many foreign missions.

Parque 3 de Febrero. 400 hectares (1000 acres) of gardens, lakes, and woods stretching along the river.

Tigre and the River Delta. Only 30 km (18 miles) outside the city, many porteños keep river houses here; Tigre itself is a lovely village and a favorite weekend destination.

Tango nightclubs. No visit to Buenos Aires would be complete without a trip to hear and dance to the country's most famous musical form.

Many of Argentina's most famous citizens are buried in the Recoleta cemetery.

Martín in Retiro and goes all the way to Palermo. Santa Fé is lined with fashionable shops. On Saturdays, you'll see very chic *porteña* women strolling along and window-shopping; in winter it's like a fur-coat fashion runway. But Santa Fé doesn't draw just the elite. Sometimes it seems as though half of Buenos Aires is cruising up and down the avenue, on their way to the movies (several of Buenos Aires's grand old movie theaters are here) or to hang out at cafés – which they do until very late at night. It's not uncommon to walk down the street at 3am on a weekday and find people of all ages still in the cafés, having a late meal or one last nightcap.

RECOLETA

La Recoleta is a neighborhood of high culture and high class. It is supremely elegant and has luxurious parks, but it is perhaps best known for its cemetery – where Evita, in the company of other illustrious *porteños*, is buried. This area was also the high ground to which the rich of San Telmo fled in the midst of the yellow fever scare of the 1870s. Today Recoleta's avenues and stately homes are the most fashion-able of Buenos Aires, though some of the newer wealth is moving out to Palermo and the northern suburbs. Buenos Aires is often cited as the Paris of South America; in Recoleta, you may actually see the resemblance.

The **Cementerio de La Recoleta**, built in 1822, is one of  the world's most impressive cemeteries. Argentina's elite – generals, presidents, and aristocrats – lie in repose here, paid tribute to by their families and loved ones in gestures poetic and flamboyant, refined and outrageous. Tiny plots of land hold mausoleums in marble and granite, adorned with protective angels and saviors. It is a high-rent city of the dead – complete with dignified tree-lined avenues and promenades, cemetery pets, and houses that make no attempt to camouflage their owners' wealth. Here you'll find Bartólome Mitre, first president of Argentina; Domingo Faustino Sarmiento, founder of the state school system in Argentina; the Paz family, which owned the legendary newspaper *La Prensa*; and Torcuato Alvear, the first mayor of Buenos Aires. Esteemed surnames and fantastic wealth are the entry requirements.

Recoleta's most famous resident, though, is Evita Perón, the beloved wife of the Argentine general Juan Perón and adopted saint of the *descamisados*, the 'shirtless' working class. To find the modest mausoleum that holds her remains,

Full of statuary and laden with bright flowers, the cemetery is a must-see.

make an immediate left after the entrance, then turn right on the large avenue. Make a left at a small alleyway with a winged angel on top of the corner – or just follow the tour groups and wait until they clear out. Halfway down the left side of the alley is the tomb, marked 'Familia Duarte' (though Evita was an illegitimate child, Duarte was her father's surname). One of the plaques on the tomb repeats

Chacarita: Buenos Aires's Other Cemetery

While Recoleta has a post-mortem lock on Buenos Aires's noble families, La Chacarita is the final resting place of some of the nation's most illustrious figures, including Juan Perón and the tango legend Carlos Gardel. More democratic than Recoleta, but in some ways just as stunning, Chacarita merits a pilgrimage if you're a tango fanatic or of the opinion that cemeteries can be beautiful, fascinating places.

Located in a northwestern neighborhood of Buenos Aires, Chacarita is easily reached by taking the Línea B of the subway to its end, the stop Federico Lacroze. The mausoleums are only slightly less grand, and you're more likely to encounter families of those buried here than tour groups. (When the location of Perón's tomb is requested of a cemetery worker, he may ask 'Are you a relative?' The fact that you are not won't stop him from pointing out the tomb.)

For Argentines, though, Carlos Gardel's tomb is the main draw. Gardel was born in France but expressed the Argentine soul through the tango. It is possible, sometimes, to find someone genuflecting in front of his tomb, which features a life-sized statue of him. Another 'saint' whose nearby tomb attracts the flowers of devotees is Madre María Salomé, known as a healer and mystic.

The Perón tomb, by the way, reads 'Tomás Perón.'

Many hundreds – if not thousands – visit Eva Perón's tomb in Recoleta cemetery each year.

her final, legendary words to her adoring throngs: 'Volveré y seré millones' (I will return and be millions).

Evita's corpse has been in Recoleta since 1976; prior to that, it had lain in waiting at the CGT *(see page 49)* and been stolen by the military and taken to Italy under a false name. It remained there until given back to her husband Juan Perón, who was living in exile in Spain, in 1971. There is some irony in Evita finding her final resting place among the Argentine elite: although she sought to enter their ranks as a champion of the working class, she also fought against them. While Evita remains a divisive figure in Argentina – people either love or loathe her memory – there is scarcely a day that her grave is without fresh flowers.

Buenos Aires Design offers luxury shopping and striking architecture.

Evita's husband, Juan Perón, is not buried in Recoleta but in Chacarita (see page 56), a cemetery more democratic but nearly as replete with works of art.

You don't really need to know the exact locations of any other grave sites. Just wander the little streets and take in the remarkable variety of architecture: Art Nouveau, Gothic, neoclassical. You'll find all kinds of surnames, especially a large number of Armenians (Buenos Aires has the largest population of Armenians outside Armenia).

Recoleta cemetery was built on the orchard grounds of the convent that had been established by the Jesuits in 1716. Thus, next to the cemetery is **Basílica de Nuestra Señora del Pilar** (Basilica of Our Lady of Pilar), a beautifully simple church that dates to 1732 and was part of the original convent of the padres Recoletos. A national historical monument, it contains outstanding examples of Spanish colonial art. Note the silver-plated altar from Alto Perú, with work done by indigenous peoples of the region.

Next door to the basilica is the **Centro Cultural Recoleta**. Originally part of the convent and its cloisters, the cultural center holds a wide variety of art exhibits, theater, and dance performances. Adjacent is **Buenos Aires Design**, an upscale mall that specializes in luxury home furnishings. You'll also find a dozen restaurants with outdoor (covered) terraces and, mostly, midday fixed-price menus.

Just outside the cultural center, the **Plaza Alvear** and **Plaza Francia** parks host dog walkers, sunbathers, human statues, and, on weekends, a 'hippie fair,' with artisanry, jewelry, t-shirts, and the like. Across from all this activity are two classic cafés, **Café de la Paix** and **Café La Biela**; while a coffee here is more expensive than anywhere else in the city, it may be a small price to pay for a window onto the genteel customs of Buenos Aires's elite. Walk west along Ortiz and you'll encounter Recoleta's Restaurant Row, chic eateries where locals and tourists meet for late-night dinners.

The high wall of Recoleta cemetery is ringed on the other side of Restaurant Row by more restaurants and, conspicuously, a series of *albergues transitorios* ('quickie' motels) and sex shows – bringing the basics of life and death into close proximity.

Palais de Glace is the yellow circular building at the foot of Plaza Alvear. This exhibition space was the first place that tango was danced in 'society.' The statue of General Alvear on horseback is one of the finest monuments in a city filled with them. Its Belgian sculptor believed so too, though he reportedly lamented that 'his greatest work was to be found among the savages of Argentina.'

As Lovely as a Tree

The green spaces of Recoleta hold some beautiful indigenous plant life. In Plaza Alvear the massive trees with branches that extend almost horizontally are *gomeros*, or rubber trees; the tall, solitary tree just outside the Recoleta Cemetery is an *araucaria*, which is found only in the southern hemisphere.

A stretch of public parks that extend to Palermo begins at the northern end of Recoleta. The **Museo Nacional de Bellas Artes** (National Fine Arts Museum), Argentina's largest and most important, is found across Avenida del Libertador from Plaza Francia. The museum possesses some 10,000 art works. Its strength is not its national collection but the works of European masters, such as Rubens, Tintoretto, Zurburán, El Greco, Goya, Rodin, van Gogh, Renoir, Monet, Modigliani, Chagall, Picasso, and Degas. Among Argentine artists, you'll find Carlos Morel, the oldest native painter in the collection, and Quinquela Martín, the master of La Boca. Large-scale temporary exhibits, cultural events, and jazz evenings are regularly hosted here.

PALERMO

Beyond Recoleta is the expansive residential neighborhood of Palermo, which jealously guards most of Buenos Aires's green space. Palermo is home to the botanical garden, horse-racing track, polo fields, city zoo, the city's largest park, the

¡Viva la Moderne!

At the point where Recoleta ends and Palermo begins is the **Biblioteca Nacional** (National Library), set back from Avenida del Libertador. This odd building, which looks like a Hollywood space ship or an A-bomb's mushroom cloud, is to some eyes hideous and others marvelous. Though conceived in the 1960s, it only opened in 1992. Dated and controversial, it is most noteworthy for the fact that it replaced a gorgeous French mansion on the site – a home in which Evita and Juan Perón lived, and Evita actually died. Before the house's demolition, one of Evita's opponents had scrawled a cruel graffito on it: '¡Viva el cancer!' (Long live cancer!). Evita, it will be remembered, died of uterine cancer.

Works of European masters and Argentine natives can be found at the Museo de Bellas Artes.

site of livestock shows, most foreign embassies, monuments, and some of the most fashionable restaurants and *boliches* (nightclubs) in the city, as well as some of its ritziest homes. The neighborhood actually comprises three areas: Palermo Chico, a very exclusive residential zone; Parque Palermo, which includes Parque 3 de Febrero and surrounding attractions; and Palermo Viejo, an interior area west of the major parks, with charming bars and restaurants and turn-of-the-20th-century *casas de chorizo* being renovated by young professionals.

The dictator Juan Manuel de Rosas, who ruled Argentina for more than three decades, was responsible for transforming the Palermo area in the 1830s from a swamp along the banks of the Río de la Plata to an area of wide spaces and parks. He built himself a mansion here to escape the pres-

Palermo Chico offers a glimpse of the high life enjoyed by wealthy porteños from the late 19th century.

sures of governing the country. When Rosas was overthrown, the zone became public park area, and gradually *porteños* moved north to take advantage of the expanse. By 1900, Palermo was already competing with Recoleta as the residential district of choice for the Buenos Aires elite.

Many French-style homes of the noble and the merely rich are found in the area known as **Palermo Chico** (Little Palermo). Today many of these homes are inhabited by foreign missions and diplomats. To get a sense of how wealthy *porteños* lived in the 1880s – and how, in isolated cases, they still live – stroll around the area. Across from the grand-looking **Museo de Artes Decorativos** (Decorative Arts Museum) is **Plaza República de Chile**, at Avenida del

Libertador and Calle Tagle. Here you'll find statues of the heroic liberators who crossed the Andes.

Across the street, the **Instituto Nacional San Martiano** exhibits national adulation in a replica of the house in the French port of Boulogne-sur-Mer where the hero San Martín died. Walk along Obarrio, Ombu, Martín Coronado, and Ocampo streets to view some of the beautiful French palaces of the wealthy families that moved north after the yellow fever epidemic of 1871. Many homes were simply too grand for heirs to maintain, although some remain in private hands. Palermo Chico is especially lovely in spring, when, as in other parts of Buenos Aires, the jacaranda trees are in full bloom and add a pretty dose of lavender to the stately ivory mansions.

On Figueroa Alcorta is the latest addition to Buenos Aires' list of museums. This is the **Museo de Arte Latinoamericano de Buenos Aires**, recognizable by its spectacular metal rose outside, which opens and shuts with the sun. The collection inside is the best of modern and contemporary art from Latin America; there are also movie showings and literary events.

Parque 3 de Febrero, also known to *porteños* as Parque Palermo or Bosque de Palermo (Palermo Forest), is where

Walking the Dog

Paseadores de perros, or dogwalkers, are a common sight in Buenos Aires parks. On weekdays in Recoleta and Palermo, crews of *paseadores* make their rounds with as many as 25 dogs, often elite breeds, in tow. (On weekends there are fewer, when owners do dog duty themselves.) But the sheer number of dogs, and the evidence they leave behind, is causing discord and discussions of mandatory clean-up laws.

This paseador de perro *(dog-walker) has his work cut out for him, thanks to Buenos Aires's strict dog-litter laws.*

the city of Buenos Aires – or at least its character as a bustling metropolis – ends. Decreed a public park by President Sarmiento in 1872, it contains gardens, lakes, and woods, and stretches along the river for 400 hectares (1,000 acres). The city's Central Park, it is a focus of porteño leisure activities; especially on weekends, you'll find cyclists, in-line skaters, joggers, soccer players, families pushing strollers, and young couples paddling boats around the lake. Within the park is the **Jardín Japonés** (Japanese Garden), a peaceful refuge with fish ponds and a Japanese cultural center; the **Rosedal**, a rose garden on Avenida Pres. Montt; and the **Planetario** (city planetarium).

At the intersection of Avenida del Libertador and Avenida Sarmiento is the bold **Monumento a los Españoles** (Spanish Monument), a 1910 gift from the Spanish government to celebrate the centennial of the May Revolution. The early 19th-century Rosas estate was near here.

Lining Avenida Sarmiento is the **Buenos Aires Zoo**, which, while not one of the world's outstanding zoos, dates to 1875 and is one of the most visited attractions in Buenos Aires. Across from the zoo is a Rodin sculpture of Sarmiento. Across Avenida Sarmiento is the **Sociedad Rural Argentina**, where the country's most important annual agricultural and livestock show has taken place since 1878.

At the end of Sarmiento is Plaza Italia; here you'll find the entrance to the **Jardín Botánico Carlos Thays** (Botanical Garden), a lovely and compact garden retreat created by the French landscaper and naturalist in the late 19th century. The garden is well-planned and maintained; it has some 7,000 species of plants – and nearly as many wild cats; the garden has become a refuge for them, encouraged as they are by the local women who feed them.

Beyond the railroad tracks in Parque Palermo is the **Hipódromo Argentino**, the racetrack where you can see some of Argentina's world-renowned thoroughbreds and jockeys in action, and, across the street, the **Campo Argentino de Polo**. Argentina is one of the world's great breeding grounds for polo players and their steeds. The arches under the railroad tracks have, in an imaginative use of space, been inhabited by bars, restaurants, and even car dealers. The strip is called **Paseo de la Infanta**, and several of Buenos Aires's most fashionable *boliches* (nightclubs) are found here. Near here is one of the city's highest structures, a 50-floor apartment building. Residents on the top floors have a view of the Río de la Plata and, on clear days, Uruguay.

The area known as **Palermo Viejo**, west of Parque Palermo, is gaining a reputation for being Buenos Aires' equivalent of

The Carlos Thays Botanical Garden is a little bit of 19th-century Paris in the middle of Buenos Aires.

New York's SoHo. While it does have a slight bohemian feel, it is nowhere near as commercial as SoHo – yet. Architects, designers, artists, and other young professionals have, since the mid-1990s, started moving in and fixing up the one- and two-story 'sausage' houses, which mostly date from between 1910 and 1930, painting them vivid colors. It is fast becoming a chic area for restaurants and evening spots. Check out the area around **Plazoleta Cortázar**, named for the great Argentine novelist and short-story writer, which has a number of colorful bars and restaurants. Businessmen with cell phones, students, and artist types all mingle here. The surrounding residential area has streets named for the Americas: Nicaragua, Costa Rica, Paraguay, Honduras, and El Salvador.

A fast-rising restaurant district, **Las Cañitas**, is just behind the polo grounds, bounded by avenidas Dorrego, Luis María

Campos, del Libertador and Federico Lacroze. The restaurants on Arévalo, Arce, and Baez are particularly lively.

The area north of Palermo along the coast, **Costanera Norte**, is a restaurant and nightlife zone, with many family-style *parrillas* and discos. In 2000, a wonderfully tacky religious theme park, the 7-hectare (17-acre) **Tierra Santa**, opened here. The park includes a recreation of Jerusalem, and has Jesus as host.

EXCURSIONS

Many people head out from Buenos Aires into the Argentine countryside to experience the great pampas, the mountains and lakes of Patagonia, or the majestic waterfalls at Iguazú. If you haven't time to do any of those splendid trips (and they take time; Argentina is huge), you can make smaller day-trips from the capital to get a taste of life beyond the porteña metropolis. You can visit the river delta and little river town of Tigre, taking the *Tren de la Costa* (coastal train); experience the extraordinarily well-preserved colonial town called, appropriately enough, Colonia, across the Río de la Plata in Uruguay; or visit an *estancia* (farm) in gaucho country.

Tigre and the River Delta

The green northern coast along the Río de la Plata is a hugely popular weekend destination for *porteños*. The riverside community of Tigre and the Paraná Delta constitutes one of Buenos Aires province's principal attractions. A short 30 km (18 miles) from the capital, the delta has just 5,500 permanent residents, but on weekends the area is invaded by more than 150,000 refugees from the city. Many *porteños* now maintain river houses out along the waterways. The delta's innumerable channels (some 1,920 km/1,200 miles of them) and islands are lush with semitropical plants. The air is clean and cool. It is excellent for river cruises, fishing, and water sports.

The **Tren de la Costa** is one of Buenos Aires's more recent touristic enterprises. A gleaming train that hugs the northern shore of the city, it traverses pleasant and rapidly growing suburbs. Each equally sparkling station along the way has been developed with consumer interest in mind: San Isidro has a giant shopping mall with restaurants and movie theaters; Barrancas, constructed in the English style out of wood, holds an antiques fair each weekend; Punta Chica has a miniature golf course. The final station, Delta, holds the biggest attraction: **Parque de la Costa**, an amusement park.

On weekends the coastal train is used by 30,000 to 40,000 people. If all this strikes you as just a little too premeditated by government tourism committees and not at all organic, you're exactly right. The train itself feels like part of the theme park. But the good news is that it gets you out to Tigre and the Delta, a lovely spot.

Tigre is a clean, white, orderly small town with wooden furniture shops and a well-known fruit market and crafts fair, the **Puerto de Frutos**. Along the riverside, on Paseo Victoria, are historic English rowing clubs, established at the end of the 19th century (though the Buenos Aires Rowing Club dates to 1758). You'll also find catamarans waiting to take visitors on **river cruises** that vary from 40 minutes to up to five or six hours. A boat trip is one of the best things you can do in the Paraná Delta. The shorter cruises along Sarmiento and Luján rivers give you only the briefest of glimpses – though you do see some of the riverside homes, where mail is delivered by boat. If you have time, it is well worth exploring further. The Dirección de Turismo near the train terminal supplies information on longer boat trips and hotels in the area. In addition, several tour companies in Buenos Aires offer Delta packages. During summer and on weekends, the region is filled with Brazilian tourists and *porteños* escaping from the city.

To get to Tigre on the Tren de la Costa, take the 'Mitre/ Suárez' train at the Retiro station (Avenida Mejía from the Torre Monumental) to the last station, Maipú (the trip lasts 30 minutes). There, cross overhead through the mall and purchase a round-trip ticket to catch the Tren de la Costa, which leaves every 10 minutes.

A longer trip, some three hours by boat from Tigre, takes you to the historic **Isla Martín García**, a former military prison camp that today is part ecological reserve, part colonial monument. Discovered in 1516, Martín García served as

Riverfront Tigre boasts a market and crafts fair, and it's a great place to begin a tour of the Paraná Delta.

a military base until the 1970s. The tiny island, comprising 180 hectares (445 acres) of natural reserve and only 200 people, is closer to Uruguay than Argentina, and has a surprisingly colorful history. Several disgraced Argentine presidents, including Juan Perón, served time here; President Sarmiento envisioned it as the capital of the Estados Unidos del Sur (United States of the South); and Rubén Darío, the famed Nicaraguan poet, wrote about it. Most people come for a daytrip, but an *albergue* and an *hostería* have opened up for those wishing to spend the night. If you visit here, it is imperative that you sample and bring back some of the island's famous *dulce de leche*, which should be purchased in the *Vieja Panadería de Martín García* (the old town bakery).

Check with the Dirección de Turismo in Tigre or directly with boats along the waterfront for trips to Isla Martín García.

Colonia, Uruguay

Just across the wide Río de la Plata from Buenos Aires is the charming historic city of **Colonia del Sacramento**. With high-speed boats departing daily from Puerto Madero, it is an easy day-trip. Passports are required to cross the border, but visas are not necessary for most nationalities. While it is certainly possible to see this serene colonial village in a day, an overnight stay in the midst of pristine colonial architecture and silent stone streets, beneath an illuminated lighthouse and antique street lamps, is relaxing and rewarding. Besides the *casco antiguo* (historic center), declared a UN-ESCO World Heritage Site, Colonia has nice beaches and forests. If you wish to see more of Uruguay, from Colonia it is just 180 km (110 miles) to Montevideo, the capital.

Colonia has a complicated history; both the Spanish and the Portuguese ruled it at different times. The town was volleyed back and forth eight times between the two colonial

A UNESCO World Heritage Site, Colonia del Sacramento is a day-trip worth everyone's while.

powers, primarily because it held strategic importance for contraband trade. Founded in 1680 by the Portuguese Manuel de Lobo, Colonia's distinctive architecture reflects its dual character. Houses of original Portuguese construction feature Spanish structural and aesthetic reforms, and vice-versa. The tiny alleyways, stucco houses, the slight inclines and descents of its streets: Colonia is a town to walk through slowly, absorbing its unique character.

The great outer wall of the original fortress was constructed in 1639, though it was destroyed in the 19th century and has since been reconstructed. A drawbridge leads to the gate (**Portón de Campo**) to the old city, which was built in 1745. Enter through the gate and turn right at the bottom of Paseo

San Miguel. The river is to your left; on your right is a charming small street with uneven stone pavement and 18th-century faded, pastel-colored houses with red tile roofs. This is **Calle de los Suspiros** (Street of Sighs). Two competing legends claim the origins of the street's name. One is that it was inspired by the final sighs of soldiers who were executed at the end of the street. The other, considerably less macabre, is that women from the town above used to sneak out and meet here with their soldier lovers from the barracks below, near the river.

At the end of Calle de los Suspiros, you'll come to the **Plaza Mayor** (main square). At the far end is the *faro* (lighthouse) and ruins of the **Convento de San Francisco**, estab-

Calle de los Suspiros, the street of sighs, is an 18th-century lane with a checkered past.

lished in Colonia just after the city's founding. The country's first Jesuit school was founded here, in 1717. On the Plaza Mayor is the **Museo Portugués** (Portugese Museum), **Museo Municipal** (town museum), **Casa del Virrey** (Viceroy's house), and **Archivo Regional** (regional archives), while down toward the water is the **Museo del Azulejo** (tile museum). All are worth stopping in for a look.

Iglesia Matriz, on Plaza de Armas, is situated at the corner of 18 de Julio and Paseo de San Antonio. Dating to 1680, it is the oldest church in Uruguay. Though it suffered considerable damage in successive battles, the church remains an attractive reminder of Colonia's history. Across Avenida General Flores is the **Museo Español**, housed in a solid mid-17th-century Portuguese structure, appropriately enough for Colonia.

A one-day package sightseeing tour to Colonia offered by **Buquebus** (Dársena Norte; tel: 11/4316-6500; <www.buquebus.com>), the bus and ferry company, is the cheapest and most convenient way to see Colonia. After lunch and a visit to the historic center, you'll be boarded on a bus and whisked off to a *granja* (farm). You may be envisioning an attractive country farm, but what you get, instead, is one of the more blatantly commercial package-tour wastes of time you'll come across. 'La Granja' is little more than an obsessive collection of cheesy kitsch, guarded inexplicably behind glass. You go all the way to Uruguay to see 'the world's second-largest collection of key chains' (over 15,000 examples), pencils, ashtrays, and other junk. The whole excursion is merely an excuse to get you into a shop selling jams, *dulce de leche*, and cheese. A few farm animals are held in pens behind the shops.

You'll then do a drive-by of **San Real de Carlos**, located 5 km (3 miles) from Colonia. This former tourist complex is

Experience life as a gaucho on the pampas with a horse-back ride over the plains.

now in ruins. It features a large bullring, hotel casino, a *frontón* (a stadium for a ball game called jai alai) , and a race-track. There is also a paleontology museum, the **Museo Municipal Real de San Carlos**. From here, it's off to the beaches for a quick dip or a visit to some mediocre hand-craft stands.

To avoid this plan, which pales in comparison to the old town of Colonia, you might feign illness after lunch and stay put. You'll have to be firm with the Buquebus tour guides, whose job it is to get you to part with your pesos. But you'll have more time to explore the colonial village, which is what you crossed the river for anyway.

Colonia is at its best in the late afternoon and early evening, when the package tourists begin to thin out. Except for weekends and summer high season, the town is especially tranquil during these hours – just a handful of visitors and locals, all of whom seem to be strolling the streets sucking on *mate* and carrying a thermos of hot water.

The Pampas

Argentina is famous for its *pampas*, and for its *gauchos*, the strong, dark, mythical cowboys of the Argentine plains. Visiting an *estancia*, one of the large farms set on the unending pampas, is a memorable experience, and more and more private *estancias* are opening their gates to visits and overnight stays. Some are as close as 60 km (35 miles) from the capital, while others are 250 km (150 miles) or more, a lengthy trip by car or bus, and a factor that should be considered when planning your trip to Buenos Aires. Should you visit one of the distant *estancias*, you should allow a good three or four days to be able to absorb the atmosphere of the pampas.

Unfortunately, it is neither inexpensive nor particularly easy to arrange the trip on your own. Your best options are

Gringo Estancias

In the past ten years, foreigners have been gobbling up cheap and incredibly rich Argentine land. Purchasing an estancia (farm) out on the Pampas has become very chic for the international jet set. It's like Wyoming, only bigger and more remote. Sylvester Stallone, Ted Turner, and the Italian owner of Benetton have all reportedly purchased *estancias*. Luciano Benetton is, in fact, said to be the largest single landowner in Argentina. He is reported to own about three-quarters of the Argentine province of Santa Cruz.

either to go through a travel agent at home or a tour operator upon arrival in Buenos Aires.

Should you wish to arrange an overnight stay at an *estancia*, you should realize that the luxury price you may pay doesn't exactly deliver luxurious comfort. These are mostly working farms; accommodations are rustic and meals simple. Some *estancias* are exquisite 19th-century estates, while others are newish houses on farm land.

Another option, if you have less time or money to dedicate to a pampas excursion, is to attend a *fiesta gaucha*, which just about every tour operator in the city and most hotels offer. These are day-long folkloric shows for tourists. Groups are bused out to the grounds of an *estancia* 60–70 km (35–45 miles) from Buenos Aires. There they are met by a group of costumed 'gauchos' (don't expect to see real gauchos) and offered appetizers of *empanadas*. Then a *parillada criolla* (barbecue) is served. The fiesta continues with traditional dancing, music, a demonstration of horseback skills, and buggy rides. Is it authentic? Will you see the working life of the classic Argentine gaucho? No and no. It's no more authentic than the dance revues of mulattas in Rio that are mere imitations of Carnival. But you'll at least get a hint of how different things outside the Argentine capital are.

☛ **San Antonio de Areco** is a good town to visit if you're interested in gaucho culture, especially if you're in Buenos Aires during the second week of November. Then you'll have an opportunity to experience *Día de la Tradición* (Day of Tradition), the grandest celebration of all things gaucho in Argentina. San Antonio de Areco, some 110 km (65 miles) west of Buenos Aires, is a small city intent on preserving its history. All buildings more than 100 years old are protected by law, and the feel of gaucho life is palpable. The town's biggest attractions are its 18th- and 19th-century buildings near the **Plaza Ruiz de Arellano**; here you'll find the **Palacio Municipal**, the **Iglesia San Antonio de Padua**, and the **Museo Ricardo Güiraldes**, a museum dedicated to the author of a classic of gaucho literature. Published in 1926, *Don Segundo Sombra (Shadows in the Pampas)* brilliantly evokes the harsh life of the gauchos and their environment. The museum has extensive grounds on the river containing numerous indigenous plants. (It is also possible to visit the Estancia La Porteña, where Güiraldes once lived.) Near the museum you can find an interesting colonial chapel, Ermita de San Antonio, an old tavern (or a restored version of one), and a 19th-century flour mill.

Everyday ranching life on the Argentine pampas.

The Day of Tradition in San Antonio de Areco is part of week-long celebration of gaucho culture, called **Semana** (or **Fiesta**) **de la Tradición**. It draws many *porteños*, so make plans early if you hope to stay in San Antonio during that time. The town is a good place to purchase gaucho artifacts and other local products, including clothing and silver.

WHAT TO DO

ENTERTAINMENT

Nights out in Buenos Aires quickly meld into the *madrugada* (morning). Lovers of late nights will find Buenos Aires much to their liking, whether those nights are spent listening or dancing to tango, hitting a *boliche* (nightclub), or going to a late film or play and adjourning to a café afterwards to discuss it. Each of those activities is a very porteño thing to do. Even weekdays, you'll see all kinds of people out at all hours of the night. No one, it seems, wants to go home.

Tango

Spain has flamenco, Brazil samba, and the US jazz. In Argentina – and more specifically Buenos Aires – one finds tango. While today tango is performed and taught all over the world, for decades true fans have made musical pilgrimages to Buenos Aires, the birthplace of the tango. A hybrid of immigrant and indigenous cultures, tango music was spawned in the 1880s. By 1920, this smoldering, unapologetically nostalgic music and its accompanying *baile* – as much mating game as dance steps – was being performed in Europe's fanciest salons.

Only a few years back, the tango had fallen from favor and descended into decadence, with only the older porteño generation continuing to practice the art. Many years of dicatorship had killed its spirit, and the 'Nuevo Tango' of Astor Piazzolla and others – tango for listening to, rather than dancing to – had created a schism between traditionalists and the avant garde. Tango became the stuff of old photos and films, something one's grandparents used to do. For a time, tango was more popular in Japan, Europe, and the US than in Argentina.

In the late 1990s, however, tango began to experience a robust renaissance. With a new audience and fresh practitioners, it is reclaiming its cultural importance at home as well as abroad. Singles and couples in their twenties crowd weekly classes in modest clubs. *Confiterías* hold weekly tango sessions for old-timers and first-timers. Tango clubs open their doors every night of the week, in virtually every neighborhood of the city. A bimonthly newsletter tracks tango happenings, and a 24-hour cable network, 'Sólo Tango,' features the pros and gives pointers to new-comers. The municipal gov-

The grace and importance of tango immortalized on El Caminito, in La Boca.

ernment sponsors tango concerts in gilded palaces. Tango in Buenos Aires is back with a vengeance.

No one can attach a specific place or year to tango's creation, but the date 11 December is annually celebrated; that's the birthday of two of tango's most revered stars, Carlos Gardel and Julio de Caro. Most believe that the music of tango was born in La Boca, the port area populated by Italian immigrants. In brothels and marginal clubs, it was played by small *orquestas* of violin, guitar, and flute. In the early 20th century, tango gained its defining instrument: the *bandoneón*, a cousin of the accordion. Tango expressed feelings of displacement; the collective nostalgia it evoked became an identifying characteristic of the porteño.

Though it began as a marginal and working-class phenomenon, tango rose from the street and *conventillos*, or tenements, and became the soundtrack for Buenos Aires's new modernity. Eventually tango conquered even the most exclusive upper-class salons, like the Palais de Glace in Recoleta. The great singer Carlos Gardel, the Frank Sinatra of tango, was largely responsible for the music's ascendancy. The original *engominado* (a nickname referring to his slicked-back hair-style) made tango romantic, not dangerous, and legitimate, rather than marginal. Elevating the *canción* (song) to an essential expression of tango, Gardel became a recording (and eventually, film) star.

The dance you'll see at clubs where regular folks dance tango is the *milonga* – traditional, deliberate tango. There is also show tango, highly choreographed 'tango for export' performed by experts. Visitors have a choice of small and smoky clubs in the bohemian neighborhood of San Telmo or high-class, high-gloss dancing and singing productions that would be at home on Broadway. At either, you'll be surprised how many tourists know the words to 'Mi Buenos Aires Querido' ('My Beloved Buenos Aires'). You can even

All About Tango

'Tango is universal.'
– Carlos Saura, Spanish filmmaker and director of the Academy-Award nominated film *Tango*
'Tango is the Argentines' most authentic cultural product.'
– Argentine writer Ernesto Sábato

A way of life, and nothing less: a musician plays his own tango in the streets of Recoleta.

see free, open-air tango at the antiques fair at Plaza Dorrego in San Telmo on Sundays or along El Caminito in La Boca. You won't have to look far for tango in Buenos Aires.

Tango is the sum of opposites: it is passionate and controlled, sensual and austere, sentimental and macho. It confidently negotiates a delicate equilibrium between harmony and resistance. Watching a live tango performance is perhaps the quintessential Buenos Aires experience. Though many shows for tourists are stylized 'tango-teatro,' all aggressive dips and splits, with legs in fishnet hose darting dangerously between knees, you'll have no trouble sensing the dark romance, melodrama, and melancholy that make the dance unique. The following is just a sampling of venues; for a list of many more, pick up the *Buenos Aires Tango Comprehensive* pamphlet distributed by Dirección General de Turismo at one of the tourist information kiosks on calle Florida.

Tango *Espectáculos* in nightclubs. Few of the original clubs where tango began exist anymore. The San Telmo *barrio* is the spiritual home of the tango; several atmospheric clubs are located there, but there are also *tanguerías*, or tango shows, in La Boca and Monsterrat (near Plaza de Mayo). Admission to shows is generally between $20 and $50; some feature open bars or include two drinks with admission. **Bar Sur** (Estados Unidos, 299, San Telmo; tel: 11/4362-6086;

The dance goes professional at the breathtaking Mr Tango Show in Buenos Aires.

<www.bar-sur.com.ar>) is a small club that has been around since the 1960s. It exudes tango ambience – which is why some 10 films have used the club as a backdrop, including the offbeat *Happy Together*. Reservations are necessary at **Señor Tango** (Avenida Vieytes, 1655, Barracas; tel: 11/4303-0231), a slick dinner show that is very well produced – enough to draw several tables of locals at every performance. **El Viejo Almacén** (Independencia at Balcarce, San Telmo; tel: 11/4307-7388) is one of the oldest *tanguerías* in town and features top talent. The same goes for **Michelángelo** (Balcarce 433, Montserrat; tel: 11/4342-7007; <www.tango show.com>). **Casa Blanca** (Balcarce 668, San Telmo; tel: 11/4331-4621) draws stars and lots of tourists to its show. **Club del Vino** (Cabrera 4737, Palermo Viejo; tel: 11/4833-0050) and **La Veda** (Florida 1, San Nicolás; tel: 11/4331-8680) are both pretty authentic and enjoy good reputations.

Tango *bailes* **and lessons.** Performances of tango can be found in several cafés and *confiterías* – authentic surround-ings in which to experience the dance. **Tortoni** (Avenida de Mayo 825), Buenos Aires's most beloved café, was once a tango haunt. It still schedules tango concerts, and houses the **Academía Nacional del Tango** (<www.anacdeltango.org. ar>) upstairs; this is a good source of information about tango events. **Clásica y Moderna** (Callao 892; open Mon–Sat, live shows Wed–Sat), an attractive, 70-year-old café, bar, and bookstore, has very good tango and jazz performances (and late-night meals).

Check also the **Salón Dorado** in the Municipal Palace on Avenida de Mayo 575 (tel: 11/4323-9669); its free concerts frequently feature tango music. Free tango is occasionally held at the **Teatro Presidente Alvear** (Avenida Corrientes 1659; <www.teatrosanmartin.com.ar>), and **Teatro Nacional Cervantes** (Córdoba 1155; tel: 11/4815-8883; <www.teatro

Try learning the tantalizing tango for yourself in the local Club Almagro.

cervantes.gov.ar>), both in the center of Buenos Aires.

For a truly porteño experience, all you need are a few pesos – and a total absence of self consciousness. Arrive at one of the following neighborhood clubs and gymnasiums early and take an informal, fun class, then stay for the action as the regulars show up. Those who arrive after 11pm are called *milongueros*. They're the traditionalists. **Club Almagro** (Medrano 522, Almagro; tel: 11/4774-7454) has classes on Tuesday, Friday and Sunday and a very good reputation. Despite the simple surroundings, Madonna and Mick Jagger have both made appearances here. **La Estrella** (Armenia 1366; tel: 11/4823-3730) is a tango dance hall staged in an Armenian social club, in a *barrio* populated mostly by Buenos Aires's Armenian Jewish community. Classes on Friday evenings at 10pm are well-attended. The *baile* afterwards is mostly tango but is punctuated by salsa, swing, and even an occasional charleston. There is a good class on Thursdays at **Niño Bien** at 8.30pm (Humberto I 1462; tel: 11/4147-8687). **Confitería Ideal** (Suipacha 380; tel: 11/5265-8069; <www.confiteriaideal.com>) is one of the city's classic confectionaries, where tango lessons are held in the main ballroom Monday–Saturday.

Performing Arts

If you have a chance to catch an opera or classical music con-
cert in the world-class **Teatro Colón** (tel: 11/4378-7132), don't
miss it. The greats have all played here – at least the greats who
visited South America. The main season is May through Aug-
ust. **Teatro Avenida**, on Avenida de Mayo 1222 (tel: 11/4381-
0662), and **Teatro Municipal San Martín**, on Corrientes 1530
(tel: 0800/333-5254), feature classical concerts and ballet.

Theater. Avenida Corrientes and the surrounding streets
hold most of Buenos Aires's theater. In most cases, you'll need
a fairly good understanding of Spanish. **Teatro Nacional
Cervantes** (Córdoba 1155; tel: 11/4815-8883; <www.teatro
cervantes.gov.ar>) and **Teatro Avenida** (Avenida de Mayo
1222) are two of the city's most prestigious theaters. **Teatro
Municipal San Martín** (Corrientes 1530) also features a variety of theater productions in its several auditoriums.

Cinema. Buenos Aires is a true movie-goer's town; it still
has a number of grand movie houses where women in full-
length furs stand in line to select their seats. There is quite a
large audience for art films. Santa Fé, Corrientes, and Lavalle
are the main streets for cinemas. **Lorca** (Av. Corrientes 1428 ;
tel: 11/4371-5017) is a good option for independent films, local
and foreign, while **Atlas Lavalle** (Lavalle 869; tel: 11/4328-
6643; <www.atlascines.com.ar>) mainly shows Hollywood
releases. Check a local newspaper for listings; foreign films are
usually in the original language and subtitled in Spanish.

Café Culture

One of Buenos Aires's most distinctive characteristics is its
café culture. A daily visit to a café is a respected ritual of life;
garrulous *porteños* treasure languid mornings and late nights at
the neighborhood café. Coffee is served the old-fashioned way:

with a pitcher of water and some shortbread biscuits or chocolate. In many cafés and confiterías, you can eat a full meal and hear some tango too. **Café Tortoni**, established in 1858 on Avenida de Mayo 825, is the kind of place you'll find yourself returning to – just like *porteños*. Jorge Luis Borges used to hang out here. It's such a classic that it had a tango composed in its honor, 'Viejo Tortoni.' It's open late, and there's a small theater and smoky billiards room in the back. The walls are lined with 2½-m (8-ft) mirrors, framed sketches, etchings, and black-and-white photos; chandeliers and giant Art-Nouveau stained-glass panels decorate the ceiling. There's even a non-smoking section, rare in an Argentine café. House specialities include desserts, *chocolate con churros*, champagne, and cider.

Confitería Ideal, in the busy microcenter at Suipacha 384, is so authentic-looking that several scenes from *Evita* were filmed among its marble columns, mahogany and mirrors.

As both patrons and waiters tend to be of the age that can say they 'knew this place when…,' **Clásica y Moderna**, in the district between Corrientes and Santa Fé at Callao 892, is aptly named. Around since the 1920s, it still feels hip and modern. It has a bookstore at the back and puts on live entertainment, during which the place feels more like a bar than a café.

Avenida Corrientes is lined with cafés. At number 1599, **Café La Paz** was the choice of intellectuals, artists, and leftists debating culture and politics, although recent refurbishment

El Café

Coffee *(café)* is served several ways: ask for a *café sólo* or *café chico* (black espresso), *cortado* (with a dash of milk or cream), or *café con leche* (half coffee and half milk). *Café con leche* is only drunk at breakfast. Coffee is often served with *medialunas* (tiny croissants, named for their half-moon shape).

While away at least one afternoon in Buenos Aires's oldest and most atmospheric café, Café Tortoni.

has sapped it of some of its atmosphere. Two of the city's most formidable cafés, haunts of the neighborhood's elite, are in Recoleta: **Café La Biela** and **Café de la Paix**, both right across from the Recoleta Cemetery and La Basílica del Pilar.

Boliches

A *boliche* can be a rowdy bar or a disco that rocks until breakfast. Among dance clubs, you can choose from a predominantly Latin bent, including tangos, salsa, merengue, samba, and *bailanta* (a local Latino rhythm previously considered 'low-class'), to international mixes reprising hits of the 1970s and 1980s, to the latest in R'n'B. Most *boliches* are open Thursday through Sunday; many have restaurants which open around 9pm, but dancing doesn't get going till 2am. *Boliches* close at 8am, just in time for breakfast. In porteño lingo, hot clubs are *in*. Many of the most fashionable *boliches* are located in the elegant *barrios* of Recoleta and Palermo. The following are currently popular, but nightclubs come and go quickly, so check the press for listings. **Crobar** (Paseo de la Infanta, Palermo) draws a young and beautiful crowd; also very trendy is **Opera Bay**, which looks to have been modeled on the Sydney Opera House (Cecilia Grierson 225, Puerto Madero). **La Morocha** (Dorrego 3307) and **Morocco** (H. Yrigoyen 851) have a wild reputation, with exotic shows, transvestites, and general hedonism. **Bahrein** (Lavalle 345) is one of the most popular spots in the city, with various types of music. **Mint** (Av. Costanera Rafael Obligado and Sarmiento, Costanera Norte; closed January), is filled with wealthy *porteños* and tourists enjoying house and techno music. Somewhat more sedate are **Hippopotamus** (Junín), and **Hard Rock Café** (Pueyrredón and Libertador), which offers live music and food. **Milíon** (1048 Paraná), built inside a stately mansion, has a lovely garden; while **Bar Seddón** (Defensa 695) is a cozy, traditional bar with live bands.

El Caminito is an open-air museum, lined with public artworks and busy with vendors selling their own masterpieces.

SHOPPING

Thanks to the 2002 devaluation of the peso, Buenos Aires has once again become something of a shopper's paradise, with prices much lower than those in North America or Europe. The best buys are products for which Argentina is especially known: leather goods, silver, and antiques. Many items are of special interest, including the gourds and *bombillas* (silver straws) that Argentines use to drink *mate*.

The main shopping streets are Avenida Santa Fé and Calle Florida. **Avenida Santa Fé** is the strolling and shopping avenue of choice for many *porteños*. Pedestrianized **Calle Florida** suffered badly in the 2001 riots and now consists mainly of cheap leather and electronics shops.

As in many cities, the focus of shopping outings has largely shifted from small shops on busy avenues to large shopping malls with controlled environments. Some of Buenos Aires's principal shopping centers include **Galerías Pacífico**, on calle Florida; **Patio Bullrich**, an elegant collection of designer shops on Avenida Libertador in Recoleta; **Buenos Aires Design Center**, also in Recoleta, for home furnishings; and **Alto Palermo Shopping**, the largest of the city's malls.

Most art galleries are located in the Barrio Norte, in Retiro and Recoleta. More popular art can be found in the weekend market on El Caminito, in La Boca.

If you're looking for books, try the grandfather of Buenos Aires bookstores, **El Ateneo** on calle Florida. Avenida Corrientes, especially the stretch between Callao and Alem, is known for its small stalls operated by booksellers.

Shopping hours are generally from 9am to 7 or 8pm weekdays and 9am to 1pm on Saturdays. Most shops close on Sundays, but the large shopping malls are now open seven days a week, usually 10am–10pm. Inquire about refunds of IVA (the value-added tax of 21%) on purchases above $70.

Antiques for sale on San Telmo's Plaza Dorrego.

Buenos Aires boasts several excellent **flea markets**. The most renowned is the *feria* in San Telmo's Plaza Dorrego, featuring antiques and other items of interest. Even if you're not looking to buy, it's a great place just to wander. Another flea market is on Avenida Dorrego in Palermo, although this gets mixed reviews, as bargains are often hard to find. The 'hippie fair' market in Plaza Francia in Recoleta on weekends is a good place to stroll and pick up inexpensive souvenirs.

Buenos Aires has an outstanding collection of European and American antiques. The main *barrio* for antiques is San Telmo; near the Plaza Dorrego, antiques shops line Defensa from Independencia to San Juan, and Estados Unidos and Balcarce also feature intriguing stores.

Stores stocking other local products and artifacts are found primarily in San Telmo and the streets in the microcenter where Barrio Norte begins: San Martín, Paraguay, Esmeralda, and Suipacha. The Sunday **Feria de Mataderos** is a festival of Argentine handcrafts and the traditional culture of gauchos and *criollos*. It features folkloric dance and music, food, and handcrafts, including ceramics, silver, wood, and textiles. If you can't make it to an *estancia*, this is a good place to see a demonstration of gaucho horseback skills. The Mataderos fair is located just a bit out of town, on Lisandro de la Torre and Avenida de los Corrales, and can be reached by bus.

SPORTS

Fútbol. Argentines are soccer fanatics, and Buenos Aires dominates the professional clubs. The two most famous soccer clubs in the city, which maintain the English names of their origins, are River Plate and Boca Juniors. The latter produced Diego Maradona, the bad boy of world *fútbol* and leader of the Argentine national team that won the World Cup in 1986. You can attend a game of either of these teams and experience the raucous support from its fans first-hand. **Estadio Monumental** is located in Núñez *barrio* (Figueroa Alcorta 7597; tel: 11/4789-1200); **La Bombonera**, the stadium belonging to Boca Juniors, is in La Boca (Brandsen 805; tel: 11/4362-2050). For information on schedules, contact the Asociación de Fútbol Argentino, tel: 11/4370-7900.

Horse racing. Argentine horses are renowned. You can catch a horse race at the **Hipódromo de Palermo** (Avenida Libertador 4205; tel: 11/4778-2800; <www.palermo.com.ar>).

Polo and pato. Two classic, elite Argentine sports, played with rare talent in both horses and men, are

La Boca, the place where fútbol reigns supreme.

polo and pato. Polo is played at the **Campo Argentino de Polo** in Palermo (Avenida Libertador at Dorrego). The game, which originated in India, was brought to Argentina by the English in the late 1800s. Buenos Aires's stadium has been around more than 100 years. Despite the game's old-money reputation, most matches are free. Contact the Asociación Argentina de Polo (Arévalo 3065; tel: 11/4777-6444) for schedules of matches.

Pato (the word means *duck*) might seem like a strange name for a field game, but once you've heard the history of the sport, you won't forget why it is so named. Indigenous to Argentina, with origins among the people and gauchos of the pampas as early as the 17th century, pato is a fusion of polo and basketball. It's played on horseback and with a leather ball with handles – a ball that once was a live duck in a leather satchel. In the course of opponents contesting for its possession and scoring baskets, the poor duck would be pummeled to death. The game was apparently violent even beyond its equipment: fallen players were routinely trampled. Pato was banned by the federal government in 1822, but the game wasn't forgotten, and a somewhat sanitized version was resuscitated a century later. Pato matches are held at the Campo Argentino de Polo in Palermo. Information is available through the Federación Argentina de Pato (Avenida Belgrano 530; tel: 11/4331-0222).

Automobile racing. Formula I and other races motor around the track at the **Autódromo de la Ciudad de Buenos Aires** (General Paz at Roca; tel: 11/4605-3333).

BUENOS AIRES FOR CHILDREN

Buenos Aires Zoo. Buenos Aires's *jardín zoológico*, or zoo, founded in the 1880s, remains a big draw for porteño children. It contains 2,500 animals, including Bengal white tigers. Privatized in the early 1990s, it is now much more lively and attractive than it once was. (Avenida Las Heras y Sarmiento, Palermo; tel: 11/4806-7412.)

Tren de la Costa and Parque de la Costa (<www.trende lacosta.com.ar>). This cute mini-train heads out into the northern suburbs along the Río de la Plata. Several of the stations along the way have been designed with families in mind, with miniature golf, movie theaters, shopping malls, roller-skating paths, and fast food restaurants among the attractions. The last stop, 'Delta,' lands you in Tigre, but more important for kids, you'll be right next to the Parque de la Costa, a theme park with shows and rides, though with pretty hefty admission prices as well. While in Tigre, children will also appreciate river *paseos* in catamarans.

Planetarium. This is a good bet with kids whose eyes glaze over at the thought of museums and historical buildings. The **Planetario Municipal Galileo Galilei** is in Pal-

In Buenos Aires, even a simple walk through the park will offer a special surprise to entertain the kids.

ermo near the Plaza Italia (Avenida Sarmiento at Roldán; tel: 11/4771-6629; open Mon–Fri 10am–6pm).

Parks and gardens. The parks of Recoleta and Palermo are especially child-friendly. The 3 de Febrero, or Parque Palermo, is full of families on weekends.

Calendar of Events

1 January	*Año Nuevo*	New Year's Day
February	*Carnaval*	Carnival
March/April	*Viernes Santo/ Pascua*	Good Friday/ Easter
April	*Feria del Libro*	Book fair
1 May	*Día del Trabajador*	Labor Day
25 May	*Revolución de Mayo*	A celebration of May 1810 Revolution
10 June	*Día de las Malvinas*	Malvinas Day
9 July	*Día de la Independencia*	Independence Day
July	*La Rural*	Agricultural Fair, Sociedad Rural Argentina, Palermo
17 August	*Día de San Martín*	Death of San Martín
12 October	*Día de la Raza*	Columbus Day
October	*Fiesta de la Tradición*	Gaucho Festival, San Antonio de Areco
October	*Fiesta Nacional de la Flor*	National Flower Festival, Escobar
25 December	*Navidad*	Christmas

EATING OUT

Argentines love to eat, and they love to eat out. Restaurants are little temples of interaction, each of its dining tables a social club. *Porteños* approach restaurants like *cariocas*, citizens of Rio de Janeiro, think of the beach: a place where life is lived. Restaurants can be very sophisticated affairs, but the classic Argentine eatery is a straightforward place for good food, good wine, and good talk.

There's something you should know about Argentines. They are carnivores the likes of which you may never have witnessed before. They slap great slabs of meat on overwhelmed plates and, amazingly, tend to finish them. It isn't out of the question for a hungry Argentine to eat steak for both lunch and dinner in the same day. Occasionally a lucky vegetable will find its way on to the plate. *Porteños* took their culinary cues from the gauchos on the pampas, who ate the meat of grass-fed cattle day in and day out. While *carne* (meat) encompasses just about everything a visitor to Argentina needs to know about dinner, two words predominate: *parrillada* (grilled meats, pronounced par-ee-*zhah*-da) and *asado* (outdoor barbecue on a spit). Mention a weekend *asado* to a porteño and watch him salivate.

International cuisine in Buenos Aires means Italian. The largely Italian-descended population eats what their ancestors ate: *fideos* (spaghetti), ravioli, *ñoquis* (gnocchi), and lasagne. International also means Chinese, and, in top-flight restaurants, French. You'll find Spanish restaurants; they're good places for fish and seafood. Many *porteños* don't seem to think all that much of fish. Even though eating options are expanding in Buenos Aires, without even trying you could spend the entire time alternating between beef, Italian, and pizza – another staple of *porteños*.

A gaucho barbecue in Buenos Aires is all about beef, as are most meals.

One of the better bargains in Buenos Aires is the midday *menú ejecutivo*, a fixed-price lunch consisting of three or four courses for around 15 pesos at many places.

Perhaps unjustly overshadowed by the products of Chilean vineyards, many Argentine wines are excellent, and they're getting better known all the time. They make excellent accompaniments to all that meat and pasta.

The restaurant scene is divided between perennial favorites that have been around for decades and a rather fickle, fashionable set that hops from *barrio* to *barrio*. A few years ago, La Costanera Norte, along the river north of town, was the hot-spot. Then it was back to Recoleta. Then the recycled warehouses on the docks at Puerto Madero were in favor. Now the *in* area seems to be Palermo Viejo, Buenos Aires's equivalent to New York City's SoHo. Fickle clients with means and a need to be in the place of the moment anoint a new area, and chefs pick up and move. Or perhaps it's the other way around. Either way, restaurants and their clients sometimes last only a year in a place before moving on.

Generally, fancier restaurants serving international cuisine and *parillada* are found in Retiro, Recoleta, Palermo, and Puerto Madero. Recoleta has two distinct restaurant rows. Some of the most chic new restaurants in the city are found in Palermo Viejo and Puerto Madero. San Telmo has a host of traditional, comfortable meat-oriented restaurants and *pizzerías*.

Argentine Cuisine

Argentine cuisine comes down, essentially, to beef. Argentines eat beef like Asians eat rice: daily. The quality of beef is world-renowned, but it is considerably less fatty than many foreigners are used to, and may take some getting used to. If you like meat, though, it won't take long.

Argentines will eat it boiled, grilled, or fried, but a wood- or charcoal-fired grill is the classic way to prepare Argentine beef. A *parrilla mixta* (mixed grill) can consist of seven or more cuts of meat, each of which you can, of course, also order individually. *Bife de chorizo* is a thick and succulent steak. *Bife de costilla* and *chuleta* are T-bones, while *bife de lomo* is a shortloin. Plain old *bife* is just a large steak.

How rare is fair?

If you're going to eat meat like a porteño, you've got to know how to order it. The standard order is *cocida*, which is well done. Few Argentines eat their meat daringly pink or red; if you like it this way, you'll have to request it clearly — rare is *jugosa*, medium is *a punto*.

Matambre is skirt steak, while *vacío* is sirloin. Accompanying major cuts of meat in a mixed grill are *chinchulines* (tripe); *mollejas* (sweetbreads); *morcilla* (blood sausage); *chorizo* (spicy pork sausage); and *riñones* (kidneys). Such a meatfest will usually come with fried potatoes and salad greens.

Besides beef, other grilled options include chicken *(pollo asado)*, young goat *(chivito)*, and suckling pig *(lechón)*. One of Argentina's great culinary creations is *chimichurri*, a tangy herb marinade ideal with choice cuts of meat.

Fish commonly served include *merluza* (hake), *trucha* (trout), and *salmón* (salmon).

Pizza isn't taken lightly in Buenos Aires; *porteños* eat pizza for dinner about as often as Americans do. Pizza in Argentina, much of it Genovese-style and made in wood

A stroll through Recoleta's streets before dinner will reveal a number of tempting restaurants.

stoves, is consistently excellent, and some of Buenos Aires's better-known restaurants are *pizzerías*.

Snacks

Some visitors to Buenos Aires swear they could subsist just on *empanadas*, the lightly baked *(al horno)* or fried *(frito)* pastry turnovers stuffed with meat and onions, chicken and egg, olives, or ham and cheese. Empanadas are frequently served as appetizers, especially in advance of an *asado* on visits to *estancias*. *Facturas* are sweet pastries, which *porteños* often gobble up in the late afternoon as an accompaniment to *mate*.

Dessert

Dessert frequently seems like an afterthought in Argentine restaurants. Often it's fresh fruit, ice-cream, or *dulce de leche*, a classic caramelized milk paste that's sickeningly sweet but quite addictive. In summer, long lines form outside the local ice-cream chains, Freddo's or new arrival Persicco's – *dulce de leche* ice-cream is especially heavenly.

Hours and Meals

Restaurants are required by law to post prices both inside and outside. Lunch *(almuerzo)* is served between noon and 2pm and may linger as late as 3pm. Restaurants open for dinner *(cena)* at 8pm, but you're unlikely to find many *porteños* eating at that hour. Some will drift in around 9pm, but many more won't sit down until 10 or 11pm. It's not uncommon for people to dine after midnight, even during the week. Breakfast *(desayuno)* usually isn't much to speak of, except in hotels that feature buffet spreads. *Porteños* might have coffee and a couple of *medialunas*, perhaps a glass of juice, but that's about it.

Tipping and Service

In restaurants, a 10% tip is customary. Some restaurants add a 'service charge' to the bill. This is not the tip, but a fee merely to sit down at a table. It may be as little as $1.50 or as much as $4.50.

Drinks *(bebidas)*

Wine *(vino)*. Argentina produces some fine wines, and *porteños*, like most Europeans, like to drink wine with their meals. Today the country ranks fifth among all wine-producing nations. Argentine wines are finally winning some acclaim internationally, but they're still not as well-known as their Chilean counterparts. Varietals (that is, wines made from particular grapes) are almost all of European extraction, having been brought over by waves of Italian and Spanish immigrants. Given the Argentines' predilection for red meat, it is not surprising that red wines predominate – and are judged by most to be vastly superior to the whites. Some experts claim that the Malbec grape has taken on unique properties in Argentina and is one of the country's great red wines.

Wines from both San Juan and Mendoza, which produce the lion's share of Argentine wines, are generally good, and potentially great. **Etchart** from Salta produces good Cabernet Sauvignon, Chardonnay, and Malbec, among others. From Mendoza, **Chandon Bodegas** produces an excellent Clos du Moulin and Comte de Valmont. The Catena Zapata Estiba Reserva from **Bodegas Esmeralda** was selected as one of the world's 100 best wines by *Wine Spectator*. Red and white wines from **Cavas de Weinert** and **Trapiche** are both consistently good, while those from **Luigi Bosca**, especially its Cabernet, are outstanding. An excellent value red is the Don Valentín Lacrado from **Bianchi Bodegas**.

¡Oye, ché¡ Pass the Mate!

Mate, or more properly *yerba mate* (pronounced 'yair-bah mah-tay') is Argentine green tea. But in Argentina this is no mere hot beverage. A practice inherited from the gauchos, the serving and drinking of *mate* has become a cultural ritual with rich social and historical significance. Though *mate* is also consumed in other Southern Cone countries, it defines Argentines nearly to the degree that the tango does. In the countryside and small cities outside of Buenos Aires, you'll see people strolling together, talking, with the *mate* (pumpkin gourd) in one hand and a thermos of hot water in the other.

You won't have *mate* in a restaurant, but if you visit *porteños* in their homes, you almost definitely will. Drinking *mate* is a demonstration of friendship and sharing. Even more than wine or other alcohol, *mate* is a social lubricant. Argentines drink several times more *mate* than coffee, and they drink it at all hours of the day.

The sharing of *mate* is a serious matter. A designated pourer, called the *cebador,* prepares the *mate* and passes it on. That person drinks all the tea in the gourd, then returns it to the *cebador,* who refills it and passes it to the next person. These rounds can go on interminably. When one has had enough, he returns the gourd, uttering a simply 'gracias' to the *cebador.* This means that he has dropped out.

In a reflection of changing times, vending machines at gas stations and convenience stores now sell pre-prepared, disposable *mates* with plastic straws. Perhaps this is a sign that even cellphone-wielding Argentines aren't ready to give up this important cultural artifact.

A *mate* gourd may be a simple calabash, an intricately carved antique silver piece that has been in the family for generations, or made from lesser materials like aluminum and wood. *Mates* and *bombillas* make excellent souvenirs; they can be found in flea markets and handcrafts shops all over town. Be sure to pick up a bag of *yerba* before you leave.

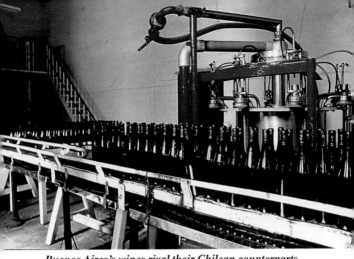

Buenos Aires's wines rival their Chilean counterparts, though they are not as well known.

Beer *(cerveza)*. Beer is widely consumed by Argentines, though it ranks a distinct second to wine among alcoholic beverages. Quilmes is a good lager beer.

Mate. *Mate*, or more properly *yerba mate* (pronounced '*yair*-ba *mah*-tay'), is Argentine green tea. *See the box on page 101.*

To Help You Order...

Could we have a table?	**Nos gustaría una mesa.**
I'd like a/an/some...	**Quiero...**

beer	**una cerveza**	cheese	**queso**
bill (the)	**la cuenta**	coffee	**café (cafecito)**
bread	**pan**	dessert	**postre**
butter	**manteca**	eggs	**huevos**

fish	**pescado**	potatoes	**papas**
fruit	**fruta**	rice	**arroz**
ice	**hielo**	salad	**ensalada**
ice-cream	**helado**	sandwich	**sanduiche**
jam	**jamón**	sugar	**azúcar**
meat	**carne**	vegetables	**legumbres**
menu (the)	**la carta**	tea	**té**
milk	**leche**	Argentine	**mate**
mineral water	**agua mineral**	green tea	
napkin	**servilleta**	wine	**vino**

...and Read the Menu

aceitunas	olives	**frito**	fried
ajo	garlic	**grillado**	grilled
albóndigas	meatballs	**helado**	ice-cream
arroz	rice	**hígado**	liver
asado	roasted	**huevo**	egg
badejo	sea bass	**langosta**	lobster
bife	beefsteak	**legumbres**	vegetables
bróculis	broccoli	**limón**	lemon
caballa	mackerel	**manzana**	apple
cabrito	goat	**naranja**	orange
camarones	shrimp	**pescado**	fish
cangrejo	crab	**pimentón**	green pepper
chinculines	tripe	**piña**	pineapple
chorizo	spicy sausage	**pollo**	chicken
chuletas	pork ribs	**postre**	dessert
coliflor	cauliflower	**queso**	cheese
cordero	lamb	**sangría**	watermelon
flan	caramel custard	**tarta**	cake
frambuesas	raspberries	**ternera**	veal
fresas	strawberries	**uvas**	grapes
frijoles	beans	**zanahorias**	carrots

HANDY TRAVEL TIPS

An A–Z Summary of Practical Information

Note: At time of printing, three Argentine pesos had the same value as one US dollar. The 'dollar sign' ($) is used to denote pesos, so 50 Argentine pesos is written as $50.

 A

ACCOMMODATION

Buenos Aires hotels, which include some of the major international chains, are of a generally high quality and steadily improving. Five years of recession and devaluation of the peso in 2002 mean that many are a real bargain. Some establishments have started a two-tier system, quoting prices in dollars.

The three major tourist areas – the microcenter of downtown, the area near the wide Avenida 9 de Julio (both in the central part of Buenos Aires), and Recoleta – are where most hotels of interest are located. In high season, October to April, hotels fill up very quickly. Reserve as early as possible for these months.

Hotels are classified by a government rating system and vary from very basic 1-star to top-of-the-line 5-star establishments; those that play host to the majority of foreign visitors are rated either 5-star (generally US$150-plus), 4-star (US$80–150) or 3-star (US$30–80). Smaller and less-expensive *pensiones, residenciales,* and *hospedajes* – businesses operated out of private homes – are not rated. *Albergues transitorios* are very cheap motels with frequent room turnover.

Prices quoted often do not include the 21% value-added tax (IVA), so be sure to inquire about this tax. Breakfast, either Continental-style or buffet, is not always included in the price.

I'd like a single/double room	**Quisiera un cuarto (una habitación) sencillo(a)/doble**
with bath/shower	**con baño privado/ducha**
with a single/double bed	**con cama sencilla/doble**
Is breakfast included?	**¿El desayuno está incluido?**
What is the nightly rate?	**¿Cuál es el precio por noche?**
Where's an inexpensive hotel?	**¿Dónde hay un hotel económico?**

Buenos Aires

AIRPORT

The international airport is **Aeropuerto Internacional Ministro Pistarini** (Argentines avoid that mouthful and call it simply **Ezeiza**, pronounced 'Ay-say-zah'; Code: EZE; tel: 11/5480-6111); it's located 35 km (22 miles) south of downtown, about a 40-minute ride. **Aeroparque Jorge Newbery** (tel: 11/5480-6111) handles domestic and regional flights (including Uruguay). It lies 3 km (2 miles) north of downtown along the Costanera, Avenida Rafael Obligado.

Taxis from Ezeiza are about $35 (pesos). Two minibus services are now available: Manuel Tienda León (tel: 11/4315-5115) and San Martín Bus (tel: 11/4314-4747). Their costs are about half the taxi fare, and can be used for hotel pickup. Allow from 45 minutes to an hour for the trip.

The airport departure tax is US$18, payable only in cash, in either US dollars or in pesos.

bus	**colectivo**
to go downtown	**al centro**
tourist information	**informaciones turísticas**
map	**plano de la ciudad**

BUDGETING for YOUR TRIP

With the 2002 devaluation of the peso, Buenos Aires has become a relatively cheap destination to visit.

Transportation to Buenos Aires. Argentina is a long way – a very long way – from Europe and North America (to say nothing of Australia, New Zealand, and South Africa). These long flights are, predictably, expensive, but you may find an off-season deal. The flight will be your major expenditure. Seek to travel outside of high season (high season is generally summer in the Southern Hemisphere, or the months October to April).

Accommodation. 5-star hotels are generally US$150-plus per night; 4-star, US$80–150 and 3-star, US$30–80. There has been a proliferation of aparthotels, which feature kitchenettes, for longer stays; they can be ideal for either business people or families on a budget. Hotels usually include breakfast but do not feature meal plans.

Meals and drinks. Dining out is a real bargain, compared to most cities in Europe and North America. A mid-day pre-fixed meal, called a *menú ejecutivo,* is widely available and a good deal. Given its quality, beef is reasonable, as are local wines – many of which are excellent.

Local transportation. Public transportation – buses and the subway, called the 'Subte' – is inexpensive. Taxis are reasonable, though locals tell visitors to count their change carefully.

Incidentals. If you plan on making any day trips from Buenos Aires, you will want to budget for transportation, whether you hire a car, take a tour or public transportation. Hotels and restaurants are generally much cheaper outside Buenos Aires. Special events – theater, opera, tango shows, and *fútbol* matches – are worthwhile additions to your budget. Tickets for these events may run from $15–30 (pesos).

CAR RENTAL/HIRE

Renting a car to get around Buenos Aires is neither necessary nor advisable. It is costly compared to taking taxis, and you're likely to spend much of your time desperately searching for a parking space. Public transportation and taxis are much more efficient and hassle-free.

If you would like to rent a car to get out of the city, Avis, Hertz, and Dollar have offices at Ezeiza airport and downtown; Budget has an office downtown but will pick up people at the airport. Argentine companies include AI Rent-a-Car and Localiza.

The minimum age is 21. Insurance *(seguro contra todo riesgo)* is required and should be included in the price. Note also that the 21% IVA (value-added tax) will be added to the cost of the car rental.

Buenos Aires

I'd like to rent a car,	**Quisiera alquilar un coche,**
today/tomorrow	**hoy/mañana**
for one day/week	**por un día/una semana**

CLIMATE

Buenos Aires is located in a mild climate zone; in winter, temperatures average 12°C (54°F), and in summer, the temperature averages 23°C (76°F), but often hovers around 32°C (90°F). Given its proximity to the Río de la Plata, you can fully expect fairly intense humidity year-round. Outside the city, temperatures are more moderate. Approximate monthly average highs and lows in Centigrade and Fahrenheit are as follows:

	J	F	M	A	M	J	J	A	S	O	N	D
Max °C	29	28	26	23	19	16	16	17	20	22	25	28
Min °C	19	19	17	13	11	8	8	8	10	13	15	18
Max °F	85	82	79	73	67	61	60	63	67	72	77	83
Min °F	67	66	63	56	51	46	46	47	51	55	59	65

Temperature

°C	-30	-25	-20	-15	-10	-5	0	5	10	15	20	25	30	35	40	45
°F	-20	-10	0	10	20	30	40	50	60	70	80	90	100	110		

CLOTHING

Porteños tend to be fairly formal – and exceedingly stylish – in their attire. If planning to go to nice restaurants, the opera, or theater, men ought to take a jacket and tie, women a dress or skirt. Dressing up is especially the norm in colder months, when women often don fur coats. In winter (ie northern hemisphere summer), a true winter coat, hat, and gloves may well be necessary.

In the summer, be mindful of Buenos Aires's humidity; shirt sleeves, shorts and sandals are *de rigueur* during the day, but in the evening, smart casual is the norm.

In any season, Buenos Aires is an excellent city to explore on foot, and this is certainly the best way to get to know individual *barrios*. Comfortable walking shoes are essential.

Argentines are very fashion-conscious; women seem to be committed to fashion that shows off their figures: *Minas* (young girls) wear their pants, especially jeans, extremely tight.

COMPLAINTS

Complaints should be brought to the attention of the Tourist Information Office (Municipalidad de Buenos Aires), Sarmiento 1551; tel: (11) 4372-3612, or the Tourist Ombudsman, Avenida Pedro de Mendoza 1835, tel: (11) 4302-7816.

CRIME and SAFETY

As major, modern cities go, Buenos Aires is still fairly safe, but since the economic crash of 2001, many more robberies have been reported. Common sense should dictate your actions. Leave major valuables and extra cash in your hotel safe; keep your wallet in your front pocket and your hand on your bag on crowded streets, and avoid deserted areas at night. Take care when hiring a taxi.

I want to report a theft.	**Quiero denunciar un robo.**
my wallet/handbag/passport	**mi cartera/bolsa/pasaporte**
my camera	**mi cámara**

CUSTOMS and ENTRY FORMALITIES

Most international visitors – citizens of the US and the UK, Canada, Australia, New Zealand, and South Africa – no longer need a visa to visit Argentina for up to three months. A valid passport is required. You will get a tourist card at the airport (or at a major border crossing). Hold on to it, as you will be required to surrender it upon departure.

Tourists may enter Argentina with up to US$10,000 without declaring the amount to customs. Anyone leaving the country with more than US$10,000 must declare it. Note that if you are entering

Argentina with laptop computers or cameras, you may have to supply a written list of those items with serial numbers, a document that will be stamped by authorities.

I have nothing to declare. **No tengo nada que declarar.**

D

DRIVING

Road conditions. If you're sticking to Buenos Aires and its immediate environs, there is little reason to drive a car. Indeed, you might risk taking your last trip if you do. Argentines usually drive on the right side of the road – they're supposed to, anyway – though you will find that they drive fast and furiously; recklessly is more accurate. Traffic accidents are the primary cause of death for people under 35 years of age, and Argentina's traffic fatality rate is one of the highest in the world.

Rules and regulations. Traffic laws and speed limits are routinely ignored – even though the latter were raised in 1995 to 120 km/h (72 mph) on highways and 130 km/h on motorways. Formal regulations require an International or Inter-American driver's license in addition to one's national or state license, though in practice authorities rarely demand such a license. They're not necessary to rent an automobile, either; one needs only a home country driver's license and an international credit card. The minimum age to rent a car is generally 21.

Liability insurance is obligatory, but reasonably priced and sometimes included in the rental price. Police routinely stop motorists at checkpoints for proof of insurance.

Fuel costs. Fuel costs are high – as are tolls outside of Buenos Aires. Distances are great, an element that should be factored into one's time and budget planning. Gasoline (petrol) is called *nafta; gas-oil* is diesel fuel. In Buenos Aires, unleaded fuel *(sin plomo)* is readily available.

Parking. Parking in downtown Buenos Aires is horrendous. Parking garages are available downtown. Parking along the street is easier in the northern neighborhoods of Recoleta and Palermo.

Fluid measures

Distance

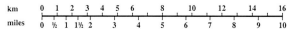

If you need help. Automóvil Club Argentino, Av. del Libertador 1850 in Palermo (tel: 11/4802-6061; <www.aca.org.ar>), has service stations and garages throughout Argentina. While one would need to become a member, the organization recognizes members of overseas affiliates (such as AAA) and entitles them to the same services and privileges.

Road Signs

Alto	Stop
Ceda el paso	Give way
Circulación	Direction of traffic
Curva peligrosa	Dangerous curve
Cuidado	Caution
Cuota	Toll
Desviación	Detour
Disminuya su velocidad	Reduce speed
Encender las luces	Turn on headlights
Escuela	School
Peatonal	Foot traffic only
Peligro	Danger
Prohibido estacionarse	No parking
Prohibido adelantar	No passing
Salida de camiones	Truck exit

Buenos Aires

Other Useful Phrases

(International) driver's license	**carnet (internacional) de conducir**
Car registration papers	**registro del automóvil**
Are we on the right road for…?	**¿Es ésta la carretera hacia…?**
Fill the tank with unleaded, please.	**Llénelo, por favor, con sin plomo.**
Check the oil/tires/ battery, please.	**Revise el aceite/las llantas/ la batería, por favor.**
I've broken down.	**El coche tiene problemas mecánicos.**
There's been an accident.	**Hubo un accidente.**
Could you fix this flat tire (puncture)?	**¿Se puede arreglar este pinchazo?**

E

ELECTRIC CURRENT

Electric current is 220V, 50 cycles. Argentina uses both the European round two-prong and the Australian slanted plugs . Adapters and transformers can be found in downtown Buenos Aires.

EMBASSIES, CONSULATES, and HIGH COMMISSIONS

Australia	Villanueva 1400; tel: (11) 4779-3500
Canada	Tagle 2828; tel: (11) 4808-1000
Republic of Ireland	Libertador 1068; tel: (11) 5787-0801
South Africa	M.T. Alvear 590; tel: (11) 4317-2900
UK	Dr. Luis Agote 2412; tel: (11) 4808-2200
US	Colombia 4300; tel: (11) 4777-4533

EMERGENCIES (See also EMBASSIES, CONSULATES, AND HIGH COMMISSIONS, HEALTH AND MEDICAL CARE, and POLICE)

The following are the 24-hour numbers to call in case of an emergency. Of course, a multilingual attendant at your hotel should be able to direct your call and explain the situation:

Police	**101**
Emergency Medical Assistance	**107**
Fire Department	**100**
Children's emergencies	**102**
Centros de Salud de Buenos Aires	**4326-6001**

I have a (medical) emergency. **Tengo una urgencia (médica).**

G

GAY and LESBIAN TRAVELERS
Buenos Aires is one of the most gay-friendly cities in South America, becoming the first city in South America to grant gay and lesbian couples the right to a civil partnership union, which allows them the same legal rights as heterosexual couples. There are particular pockets within the city where gay and lesbian life is centered, including Plaza de Recoleta, Plaza Dorrego in San Telmo, and the areas around the Avenidas Santa Fé, Corrientes, and Florida.

GETTING THERE

Air travel. From North America, most flights depart from New York, Miami, and Los Angeles. American Airlines flies direct from New York and Miami. Aerolíneas Argentinas has flights from major international destinations.

Montréal and Toronto are the major gateways in Canada. The major national airlines fly to Buenos Aires from Europe, although it is often less expensive to go via New York or Miami. Flights from Asia generally go through North America. The Brazilian airlines make stops in Rio and São Paulo, while many flights from South Africa also make stops in Brazil before going on to Argentina.

Buenos Aires

International airport. Aeropuerto Internacional Ministro Pistarini, called simply 'Ezeiza' (tel: 11/5480-6111), is located about 35 km (21 miles) south of downtown *(see page 106)*.

Air passes. Aerolíneas Argentinas offers a 'Visit Argentina' air pass for discounted travel within Argentina. Passes cost less if you fly Aerolíneas Argentinas to Argentina than if you fly with another carrier. Air passes must be purchased outside Argentina. Austral and LAPA airlines also offer air passes. See <www.aerolineas.com.ar> for fare structure and a list of overseas offices.

GUIDES and TOURS

The Municipal Tourism Office (Sarmiento 1551, 5th floor; tel: 11/4374-1251) offers free, guided neighborhood city tours, by foot or by bus, on weekends. Call for schedules.

I'd like an English-speaking guide, please.	**Quisiera un guía que hable inglés, por favor.**
I need an English interpreter.	**Necesito un intérprete de habla inglesa.**
At what time does it begin/end?	**¿A qué hora empieza/termina?**

HEALTH and MEDICAL CARE

The water in Buenos Aires is drinkable. If you confine yourself to the capital and its environs, you should encounter no major health risks.

Buenos Aires's public hospitals are usually good and free of charge. Nevertheless, it is still essential to be fully insured before traveling.

Major hospitals include:

Hospital Alemán, Av. Puerreydón 1640; tel: 11/4827-7000; <www.hospitalaleman.com.ar>.

Hospital Británico, Perdriel 74; tel: 11/4309-6400

Hospital Municipal Juan Fernández, Av. Cerviño 3356, Palermo; tel: 11/4808-2600

The following tourist health services are also available:

Assist Card   Suipacha 1109; tel: 11/4312-6801
Universal Assistance   Av. Córdoba 967; tel: 11/4323-6000
Sur Assistance   Av. Córdoba 1367; tel: 11/4814-4372

Many pharmacies can be found downtown; they operate a rotating schedule through the night. Every pharmacy should have posted a list of the nearest pharmacy open for after-hours attendance that day.

For emergency medical assistance, call tel: **107**.

| I need a doctor. | **Necesito un médico.** |
| Where is the closest hospital/pharmacy? | **¿Dónde está el hospital/ la farmacia más cercano(a)?** |

LANGUAGE

The official language in Argentina is Spanish, although a few indigenous languages are also spoken. You are unlikely to hear these, however, in the capital or its immediate environs.

Argentine Spanish is distinctive among New World Spanish. They call it *castellano* (Castilian), but *argentino* is what locals should really ly call their *español*. Most Latin Americans can imitate its exaggerated inflections and idiosyncratic use of the form *vos* (second person singular), in place of the *tú* used throughout Latin America and Spain. For example, the phrase 'Are you eating?' instead of '¿Tú comes?' in Argentina becomes '¿Vos comés?' Argentines do not, however, employ Spain's *vosotros* form for third-person plural; they use the *Uds.* ('you all') common to Latin America, which can be either formal or informal.

The double 'l,' as in 'parrilla,' and the letter 'y,' as in 'playa,' are pronounced not 'yeh' but 'zh' – as in the word azure. Those words become 'par-*ee*-zha' and '*ply*-zha.' As opposed to Spain, but as is common in Latin America, the letters 'c' and 'z' are pronounced the same, like 's' in English.

Argentine slang is called *lunfardo (see page 13),* a widespread and colorful means of expression.

Buenos Aires

Basic phrases

Good morning/good day	**Buenos días**
Good afternoon/evening	**Buenas tardes**
Good night	**Buenas noches**
hello	**hola**
goodbye	**adiós**
I don't understand.	**No entiendo.**
See you later.	**Hasta luego.**
Please	**Por favor**
Thank you	**Gracias**
How much is it?	**¿Cuál es el precio?/¿Cuánto es?**
To the hotel, please.	**Al hotel, por favor.**
To the airport, please.	**Al aeropuerto, por favor.**

Days of the week

Sunday	**domingo**
Monday	**lunes**
Tuesday	**martes**
Wednesday	**miércoles**
Thursday	**jueves**
Friday	**viernes**
Saturday	**sábado**

Months

January	**enero**
February	**febrero**
March	**marzo**
April	**abril**
May	**mayo**
June	**junio**
July	**julio**
August	**agosto**
September	**septiembre**
October	**octubre**
November	**noviembre**
December	**diciembre**

Numbers

1	**uno**	16	**dieciséis**
2	**dos**	17	**diecisiete**
3	**tres**	18	**dieciocho**
4	**cuatro**	19	**diecinueve**
5	**cinco**	20	**veinte**
6	**seis**	30	**treinta**
7	**siete**	40	**cuarenta**
8	**ocho**	50	**cincuenta**
9	**nueve**	60	**sesenta**
10	**diez**	70	**setenta**
11	**once**	80	**ochenta**
12	**doce**	90	**noventa**
13	**trece**	100	**cien**
14	**catorce**	500	**quinientos**
15	**quince**	1,000	**mil**

MAPS

Good pocket maps are available in Spanish and English from one of the municipal tourism kiosks in downtown Buenos Aires. These are located at Avenida Pte Quintana 596 (Recoleta); Defensa 1250 (San Telmo); Torre Monumental, Florida 100 (Retiro); Avenida Alicia Moreau de Justo 200 (Dock 4, Puerto Madero); and Retiro bus station.

Do you have a city map?	**¿Tiene un plano de la ciudad?**
country map	**mapa del país**
regional map	**mapa regional**

MEDIA

The Buenos Aires Herald, published in English, is a daily newspaper available at kiosks throughout the city. You will also find *The*

Buenos Aires

International Herald Tribune. Argentina's principal newspapers are
La Prensa, La Nación, and *Clarín.*

CNN, BBC, and Sky are widely available in most hotels with satellite dishes. One local cable station of interest is Sólo Tango, a 24-hour tango station.

Do you have a newspaper in English?	**¿Tiene un periódico (diario) en inglés?**

MONEY MATTERS

Currency. The national currency, the **peso**, was pegged to the US dollar at a rate of one to one in 1991, in an attempt to combat the inflation that perennially plagued Argentina. (In 1989 the annual rate reached 5000 percent.) In early 2002, the peso's parity with the US dollar was ended and the Argentine currency was devalued by nearly 66 percent. The country is therefore currently a relatively cheap place to visit. Notes are available in denominations of 2, 5, 10, 20, 50, and 100 pesos. Like the dollar, the peso is divided into 100 centavos; coins in circulation are 5, 10, 25, and 50 centavos, and one peso.

Currency exchange. US dollars are the preferred foreign currency, and they may easily be exchanged in major banks and exchange houses *(casas de cambio)*. Most banks are located downtown along Corrientes, Suipacha, and Avenida 25 de Mayo. Dollars are also widely accepted as payment. Exchange houses abound along San Martin, Florida, and Corrientes. If you are exchanging any currency other than dollars, you should proceed to a *casa de cambio*, as most banks trade only in dollars and pesos. Unlike the practice in some countries, exchange houses usually give the prevailing rate without charging commission. In addition to a major credit card, travelers are advised, if they can, to bring a small amount of cash in US dollars, which prove easier to exchange on holidays.

Banking hours. Banks are open Monday to Friday from 10am to 3pm, while *casas de cambio* are generally open Monday to Friday from 10am to 5 or 6pm.

Credit cards. Major credit cards, including Visa, MasterCard, American Express, and Diners, are widely accepted. In some cases, a minimum charge is required. Some stores have been known to add a 10% fee to purchases made with credit cards. Cash advances on Visa and MasterCard are possible at downtown banks between the hours of 10am and 6pm.

ATMS. ATM machines are now found throughout Buenos Aires; they dispense currency in pesos. Cirrus, Plus, and Link networks are all present.

Travelers checks. Travelers checks are easily exchanged in major banks and *casas de cambio*, though usually with a small service charge.

bank	**banco**
I'd like to change some dollars/pounds	**Quisiera cambiar dólares/libras.**
What's the exchange rate?	**¿A cuánto está el cambio?**
Do you accept credit cards/ travelers checks?	**¿Se aceptan tarjetas de crédito/ cheques de viajero?**
How much is it?	**¿Cuánto es?**
Do you have anything cheaper?	**¿Tiene algo más barato?**

OPENING HOURS

General business hours are 9am–6pm. Banks are open 10am–3pm. Stores are open 9am–8pm, though in some areas they may close for siesta from 1–4pm, and Saturdays 9am–1pm. Shopping malls are open daily 10am–10pm. Most museums are closed on Mondays; their hours are generally Tuesday–Sunday 10am–5pm.

Argentines tend to dine nearly as late as Spaniards. While restaurants open for lunch at noon, most people eat later, at 1 or 2pm. You can eat dinner starting at 8pm, but most Argentines won't sit down for a dinner in a restaurant, even on a weeknight, before 10pm. Restaurants may be hopping well after midnight. Most restaurants do not stay open between the lunch and dinner hours. *Boliches* (nightclubs) stay open very late, often until 8am.

At least in the Buenos Aires area, the mid-day siesta is almost completely nonexistent.

What time do you open/close?   **¿A qué hora se abre/se cierra?**

POLICE (see also CRIME AND SAFETY and EMERGENCIES)

The police may not prove especially helpful, especially if your Spanish is limited. If you need assistance, you might try one of the municipal tourism kiosks (see TOURIST INFORMATION OFFICES). The police emergency number is **101**. The Central Police Station is located at Moreno 1550; tel: (11) 4383-5051. The Tourist Police offer assistance in several languages and are located at Avenida Corrientes 436, tel: 0800/999 5000.

police   **policía**

POST OFFICES

Argentine mail was privatized and has improved in recent years, but you should still lower your expectations in terms of efficiency or dependability. Strikes and work stoppages are common, as are lost letters. Despite the inadequacies, mail rates are among the highest anywhere. An international letter of 20 grams or less outside the Americas costs $1.50.

The main post office (Correo Argentino) is located at Sarmiento 151; it's open weekdays 9am–8pm, Sat 8am–1pm.

stamp	**estampilla**
air mail	**correo aéreo**
registered	**registrado**
express delivery	**urgente**
how long will it take?	**¿Cuánto demorará en llegar?**
I'd like to send this letter	**Me gustaría enviar esta carta.**

PUBLIC HOLIDAYS

1 January	*Año Nuevo* (New Year's Day)
March/April	*Viernes Santo* (Good Friday)
1 May	*Día del Trabajador* (Labor Day)
25 May	*Primer Gobierno Patrio* (Commemoration of 1st Government/Anniversary of the May 1810 Revolution)
10 June	*Día de la Soberanía Nacional* (Malvinas Day, shifted to previous Monday)
20 June	*Día de la Bandera* (Flag Day)
9 July	*Día de la Independencia* (Independence Day)
17 August	*Aniversario de la muerte del Gral. San Martín* (Anniversary of the Death of San Martín)
12 October	*Día de la Raza* (Columbus Day)
8 December	*Día de la Inmaculada Concepción* (Day of the Immaculate Conception, shifted to previous Monday)
25 December	*Navidad* (Christmas)

holiday	**día festivo**
Will it be closed?	**¿Estará cerrado?**

PUBLIC TRANSPORTATION

Bus. *Colectivos* go everywhere in the city – but grasping their routes will prove pretty complicated on a short stay. Around 150 different lines circulate in the Capital District, running 24 hours a day. Your best bet is to inquire with locals at the nearest newspaper stand; *porteños* tend to be very well informed when it comes to bus routes and numbers. A small pocket guide to all the bus routes in the capital, called the 'Guia T', is available for a few pesos from any newsstand. Most of the colorful old *colectivos*, which look as though they've been plucked from Mexican mining towns, are no longer in circulation.

Subway. Called the *Subte* (pronounced 'soob-tay,' for 'Subterráneo,' or underground), the oldest subway system is Latin America (begun in

1913) is the best and cheapest way to make your way around the city. Most rides take no more than 20 minutes. Lines A (the oldest), B, C, D, and E operate weekdays and Saturdays from 5am–10pm, and Sundays and holidays from 8am–10pm. The cost is 70 centavos.

Trains. Trains will be most useful for trips to Tigre or La Plata. To get to the former, the 'Mitre/Suárez' train originates at the Retiro train station (Avenida Mejía across from the Torre de los Ingleses), and the *Tren de la Costa* leaves from Estación Maipú. The only long-distance train runs from Buenos Aires to Mar del Plata. Main train stations are Retiro, Constitución, and Once (pronounced *ohn*-say). For more information, check with the municipal and national tourism offices.

bus	**colectivo**
catch a bus	**tomar un colectivo**
taxi driver	**taxista**
Where does this (bus/train) go?	**¿A dónde va este tren/colectivo?**
How much is the fare?	**¿Cuál es la tarifa?**
car	**auto**

R

RELIGIOUS SERVICES

The official state religion, Roman Catholicism, has lost some territory to evangelical Protestantism, as is the case elsewhere in South America. But the Catholic Church remains one of the fundamental institutions of Argentine society. Principal saints' days and other religious holidays are celebrated with continuing dedication; almost everything is closed on Sunday. Other religious communities, from Jewish to Muslim, are well represented in the city.

T

TELEPHONES

Argentina's country code is **54**. To dial Buenos Aires from abroad, dial your international access code + **54** + **11** (city code) + number.

The best option for making long-distance calls is to go to a privately operated *locutorio*; from private booths you make your call and pay afterwards. You can usually send international faxes here as well. You may also make collect and credit card DDI – International Direct Dialing – calls with home-country operators. Be warned, however, that few *locutorios* will allow you to make calling card or DDI calls, since they stand to make nothing on such calls. You can try the Telefónica office at Corrientes 701 for credit-card calls and connections with foreign operators. The office is efficient and open 24 hours a day.

To use public phones on the streets, you can use coins or purchase set-value calling cards *(tarjetas)* at kiosks or *locutorios*. Rather than dealing with feeding coins into the machine, you should opt for more convenient phone debit cards, sold in 25, 50, 100 and 150 *ficha* amounts. To make a local call, simply dial the number. To make an international call, dial **00** + country code + number, or dial **000** for the international operator.

The cost of making international phone calls from Argentina is exorbitant. You should look into bringing a calling card from your home country, along with the company's access code for Argentina. Hotel surcharges on international calls can be equally outrageous, perhaps enough to make you forget you've got friends and family back home.

The Argentine state phone system was once one of the world's worst. In the late 1980s, people occasionally had to wait days to place an international call, while residents sat on wait-lists for months and sometimes years hoping merely to be awarded with phone service. Apartments for sale *with* telephones were especially coveted. However, since the privatization of the national phone system the service has become much more efficient and the line quality is high. Two companies, Telecom and Spanish Telefónica, service the country, splitting Buenos Aires down the middle. Despite the improvements, telephone bills are still extremely high relative to the service provided, and many Argentines prefer to use cellphones as their sole means of telecommunications.

Buenos Aires

Country codes: US (1); UK (44); Ireland (353); Canada (1); South Africa (27); Australia (61); New Zealand (64).

collect call	**cobro revertido**
operator	**operador(a)**
debit card	**tarjeta**
token	**ficha/cospel**
I'd like to make a phone call (international)	**Me gustaría hacer una llamada (internacional).**

TICKETS

Tickets for theater and films, often discounted, are available at several agencies on Avenida Corrientes. You can also try Cartelera Lavalle, Lavalle 742; tel: 11/4322-1559; <www.123info.com.ar>.

TIME DIFFERENCES

For most of the year (except during Daylight Savings Time, October to April), Argentina is three hours behind Greenwich Mean Time (GMT).

New York	Argentina	London	Jo'burg	Sydney	Auckland
7am	9am	12pm	1pm	9pm	11pm

TIPPING

In restaurants, tip about 10%. Hotel porters are generally tipped about US$1 per bag. Taxis need not be tipped. Theater or movie ushers are usually given a few small coins.

Is the tip included?	**¿Está incluida la propina (el servicio)?**

TOILETS

For public toilets, your safest and most convenient option is to use those in cafés and restaurants. The sign 'WC' is frequently used to designate public restrooms.

Where is the toilet?	**¿Dónde está el (cuarto de) baño?**

TOURIST INFORMATION OFFICES

In advance of your trip, you may write or visit an Argentine consulate or tourism office for information, or look at their website.

Australia	1–13 Alfred Street Circular Quay, Sydney 2000; tel: (612) 9251-3402; <www.argentina.org.au> 3rd Floor, Suite 102, MLC Tower, Woolen ACT 2606, Canberra (PO Box 262); tel: (6162) 82-4555
Canada	90 Sparks Street, Suite 620, Ottawa, Ontario KIP 5B4; tel: (613) 236-2351; <www.argentina-canada.net> 2000 Peel Street, Montréal, Québec H3A 2W5; tel: (514) 842-6582
New Zealand	Level 14, 142 Lambton Quay, Wellington; tel: (64) 4472-8330; <www.arg.org.nz>
South Africa	200 Standard Plaza, 400 Hilda Street #0083, Hatfield, Pretoria; tel: (27) 1243-3526
UK	65 Brook Street, London W1Y 1YE; tel: (020) 7318-1300; <www.argentine-embassy-uk.org>
US	12 W 56th Street, New York, NY 10019; tel: (212) 603-0443; <www.congenargentinany.com>

Once in Buenos Aires, you can visit the municipal tourism office, the Dirección General de Turismo (Municipalidad de Buenos Aires) in the Centro Cultural San Martín, Sarmiento 1551, 5th floor (tel: 11/4372-3612); or the Dirección Nacional de Turismo, Santa Fé 883 (tel: 11/4312-2232 or 0800/555 0016).

There are also tourist information offices at both Ezeiza International and Jorge Newbery airports. Probably most convenient for most visitors are the tourism kiosks in the city center: Avenida Pte Quintana 596 (Recoleta); Defensa 1250 (San Telmo); Torre Monumental, Florida 100 (Retiro); Avenida Alicia Moreau de Justo 200 (Dock 4, Puerto Madero); and Retiro bus station.

The English-language *Buenos Aires Herald* is a good source of information on where to visit. The newspaper also has a website: <www.buenosairesherald.com>

WEBSITES AND INTERNET CAFES

Information on tourism in the city, including museum details, can be found at **<www.buenosaires.gov.ar>**, which is in English as well as Spanish. There are several Argentina sites that have information relevant to visitors to Buenos Aires; try **<www.Argentina.com>**, although it is in Spanish. The Argentine Secretary of Tourism maintains a website at **<www.turismo.gov.ar>**, which is in English. For information on all the capital's museums (Spanish only) go to **<www.museos.buenosaires.gov.ar>**.

The internet can be accessed throughout the country. Connections are particularly good in cities, and rates in Buenos Aires are the cheapest, at only a few dollars an hour. Outlets come and go but there are some big chains, where you can sip coffee and listen to music as you surf, as well as connections at larger airports and railway stations.

WHEN TO GO

Argentina offers most North American and European travelers a delightful exchange: hitting summer in the middle of their winter, or going south for skiing in the middle of summer. Buenos Aires is fine year-round, though at its best in spring and autumn. During the Argentine summer, *porteños* flock to the beach at Mar del Plata. While it's not a bad time to be in the capital, it's not ideal if you were hoping to make – like all those capital-city residents – an excursion to the beach.

YOUTH HOSTELS

With over 100 backpackers' hostels in the city, there is no shortage of budget accommodation, and dormitory beds are available from US$7 per night. Click on to the Hostelling International website at **<www.hostels.org.ar>** for a list of hostels and an online booking service. The Albergue Buenos Aires Esther Naidemheim at Brasil 675 is the largest in the city, with 90 beds.

Recommended Hotels

Buenos Aires hotels are of a generally high international level, and currently represent excellent value for money. The major tourist areas – the area near the wide Avenida 9 de Julio, the center, and Recoleta – are where most hotels of interest are located. There is a general shortage, particularly of 4- and 5-star establishments, so make sure you arrive with reservations, in particular druing high season (October through April). If you arrive without having booked, the *turismo* desk at the airport can be of assistance.

Prices quoted often do not include the 21% value-added (IVA) tax. Be sure to inquire whether the rate you have been quoted includes this tax. Breakfast, either Continental or buffet, is not always included in the price. All the hotels listed below accept major credit cards.

Argentina's country code is 54; the city code for Buenos Aires is 11.

$$$$	over US$150
$$$	US$80–150
$$	US$30–80
$	under US$30

Avenida 9 de Julio and Congreso

Bristol Hotel $$ *Cerrito 286; tel: (11) 4382-5400; fax: (11) 4382-3284.* This traditional hotel, now some 40 years old, has been well maintained, and the service is excellent. Internet access in all rooms. It's located in the shadow of the obelisk and only a few blocks from the Teatro Colón. 125 rooms.

Carlton Hotel $$$ *Libertad 1180; tel: (11) 4812-0080; fax: (11) 4812-0081.* On the fringe of Recoleta, the Carlton offers good value for money. It features comfortable, nicely decorated rooms with all modern amenities and good service. The location is ideal for nightlife options in Barrio Norte, along Santa Fé, or in elegant Recoleta. 82 rooms.

Conte Hotel $$$ *Carlos Pellegrini 101; tel: (11) 4326-8898; fax: (11) 4394-5492.* A modern hotel just off 9 de Julio in Monserrat, the Conte is within strolling distance of Avenida de Mayo. Rooms are standard but comfortable. Business equipment is available for rent. 118 rooms.

Crowne Plaza Panamericano Buenos Aires $$$$ *Carlos Pellegrini 551; tel: (11) 4348-5000; fax: (11) 4348-5250; <www. crowneplaza.com.>.* Within shouting distance of the Obelisco on 9 de Julio, this modern hotel is popular with upscale groups and conventions, as well as a popular spot for banquets and receptions. It's just a couple of blocks to the Teatro Colón and excellent shopping and nightlife options. Rooms are classically decorated. The restaurant and pool are among the city's finest. Wheelchair access. 376 rooms.

Gran Hotel Colón $$$$ *Carlos Pelligrini, 507; tel: (11) 4320-3500; fax: (11) 4320-3507; <www.colon-hotel.com.ar>.* Facing the Obelisco on 9 de Julio and just two blocks from the Teatro Colón, the location is very convenient and the rooms not as noisy as one might fear, given the amount of traffic on the main thoroughfare. Service is excellent, and rooms are very comfortable. The suites are extremely spacious, but standard rooms a bit small. The clientele is a mix of business travelers and tourists from around the world. Don't miss the excellent buffet breakfast. Rooftop pool. 208 rooms.

Hotel Regente Palace $$$ *Suipacha 964; tel: (11) 4328-6800; fax: (11) 4328-7460; <www.regente.com>.* Between the microcenter and Barrio Norte, this pleasant hotel is a comfortable option among affordable hotels. Rooms are decorated in restful colors and available with a choice of beds. The hotel has its own car service. 150 rooms.

Hotel República $$ *Cerrito 370; tel/fax: (11) 4382-5050; <www.hotelrepublica.com.ar>.* With views like a Buenos Aires postcard – of the obelisk and 'the world's widest avenue' – the hotel is great for business people on a budget as well as families. Rooms aren't large, but they can be connected. Noise-proof windows shut out the commotion of 9 de Julio. The hotel's health club is excellent, but costs extra. Wheelchair access. 209 rooms.

Puerto Madero

Faena Hotel and Universe $$$$ *Marta Salotti 445, Digne 2, Madero Este; tel: (11) 4010-9000; fax: (11) 4010-9001; <www.faenahotelanduniverse.com>*. This hotel is a new landmark in Buenos Aires. Built from the shell of an English-style wharf, it is one of the city's most luxurious, all-inclusive hotel complexes. Includes two restaurants, a bar, pool and a cabaret show every Friday night. 106 rooms.

Hilton Buenos Aires $$$$ *Macacha Güemes 351, Digne 3, Madero Este; tel: (11) 4891-0000; fax: (11) 4891-0001; <www.hilton.com>*. Built in the rejuvenated area of Puerto Madero, this hotel is popular with affluent couples and business conventions. The building itself is stunning and many rooms offer great views over the docks. One of best hotel pools in the city. 418 rooms.

Hotel Madero $$$$ *Rosario Vera Peñaloza 360; tel: (11) 5776-7777; <www.hotelmadero.com>*. Part of the Sofitel chain, with 198 rooms, a stunning restaurant, and highly recommended bar.

Microcenter/Retiro/Barrio Norte

Aspen Suites $$$ *Esmeralda 933; tel: (11) 4313-9011; fax: (11) 4313-8059; <www.aspensuites.com.ar>*. This aparthotel, well-located near principal shopping and business areas, has a number of room options, making it a good choice for business travelers and families. Some rooms can accommodate as many as six people. All rooms have kitchenettes, but their total size as well as the sizes of the individual rooms varies, so request to see one before you make a commitment. The aparthotel is run by the management of the Aspen Towers Hotel. 148 rooms.

Aspen Towers Hotel $$$$$ *Paraguay 857; tel: (11) 4313-1919; fax: (11) 4313-2662; <www.aspentowers.com.ar>.* This sleek hotel is outfitted with everything a business traveler might need. Rooms are elegant suites with noise-proof windows; the location is within walking distance of Plaza San Martín and the financial district; and the business center is excellent. The breakfast buffet is notable. 75 rooms.

Bisonte Hotel $$$ *Paraguay 1207; tel: (11) 4816-5770; fax: (11) 4816-5775.* A good-value, modern hotel with a fine microcenter location and excellent views, the Bisonte offers everything you need for a relaxed stay. Rooms are not large but they are comfortable, and the breakfast buffet may allow you to skip lunch. 90 rooms.

Bisonte Palace Hotel $$$ *Marcelo T. Alvear 910; tel: (11) 4328-4751; fax: (11) 4328-6476; <www.hotelesbisonte.com>.* Another modern hotel located on a busy corner near the Plaza de San Martín and 9 de Julio, this is a favorite of business people. Rooms are smallish but clean. The hotel is pleasant and recommended by repeat visitors. 66 rooms.

Dolmen Hotel $$$ *Suipacha 1079; tel: (11) 4315-7117; fax: (11) 4311-5666.* Just a few blocks up Santa Fé from Plaza San Martín, this hotel in the microcenter is good value. It offers excellent service and luxury for well below the price of other top hotels. It features well-designed rooms, a health club, and business center. Wheelchair access. 146 rooms.

Gran Hotel Buenos Aires $$$ *Marcelo T. Alvear, 767; tel: (11) 4312-3003; fax: (11) 4315-2243.* A stylish hotel not far from Plaza San Martín, this is a good option for staying near the center at a reasonable price. Rooms are not huge, but they are certainly comfortable. Offices are available for business travelers. 100 rooms.

Hotel de las Américas $$$ *Libertad 1020; tel: (11) 4816-3432; fax: (11) 4816-0418; <www.grupoamericas.com.ar>.* Located in residential Barrio Norte, with easy access to the chic shopping area of Santa Fé and the microcenter, this is a very comfortable and popular hotel. Rooms are handsomely decorated, as are the spacious bathrooms. Tour groups, many from other parts of South America, frequent the place. 165 rooms.

Hotel Claridge $$$$ *Tucumán 535; tel: (11) 4314-7700; fax: (11) 4314-8022; <www.claridge.com.ar>*. The elegant and charming Claridge has a reputation for being very British. Rooms are luxuriously decorated and spacious. Quite near the financial district and shops, the Claridge attracts both business travelers and tourists. The namesake restaurant is recommended, as is the well-equipped health club. Outdoor heated pool. 157 rooms.

Hotel Continental $$ *Avenida Saenz Peña 725; tel: (11) 4326-1700; fax: (11) 4322-1421*. In Montserrat, equidistant from the Plaza de Mayo and the obelisk, the Continental is well situated and reasonably priced. Housed in one of the neighborhood's French fin-de-siècle buildings, its rooms are large and comfortable. Internet access, swimming pool, and fitness center. 160 rooms.

Hotel Crillon $$$ *Santa Fé 796; tel: (11) 4310-2000; fax: (11) 4310-2020*. In an elegant *barrio* ideal for shopping and sightseeing, the Crillon, built in 1948, stands out. It's also excellent for business travelers. Executive services, including the business center, are quite good. The top two categories of rooms are well-decorated and comfortable. Those in front have nice views and light. Both executive and family suites are available. 96 rooms.

Hotel Inter-Continental Buenos Aires $$$$ *Moreno 809; tel: (11) 4340-7100; fax: (11) 4340-7199; <www.intercontinental. com>*. In a historic part of town, near the Plaza de Mayo and Manzana de las Luces, this is one of the city's newest luxury hotels. Large and elegant rooms have views of the river. The 'Inter' has a covered pool, a good restaurant called Mediterraneo, and excellent business facilities. Wheelchair access. 315 rooms.

Hotel Lancaster $$ *Córdoba 405 and Reconquista, Retiro; tel: (11) 4311-3021; fax: (11) 4312-4068; <www.lancasterhotel-page.com>*. A very cozy option in the center of the hustle and bustle of the city. Well-equipped rooms and friendly service come at a decent price. It's best to reserve a room on the higher floors above Tres Sargentos as these tend to be the quietest.

Hotel Phoenix $$ *San Martín 780; tel: (11) 4312-4845; fax: (11) 4311-2846.* This well-located hotel in a handsome Art Nouveau building offers service you wouldn't expect at this price or in this location. It's next door to Galerías Pacífico. The rooms themselves are acceptable. 53 rooms.

Loi Suites Arenales Hotel $$ *Arenales 855; tel: (11) 4311-3929; fax: (11) 4312-1472; <www.loisuites.com/arenales>.* With a location near Plaza San Martín in Retiro, this comfortable and contemporary aparthotel is a bargain. Rooms, which can accommodate up to 3 people, have well-equipped kitchenettes, and there's a small informal restaurant in the lobby. 86 rooms.

Marriott Plaza Hotel Buenos Aires $$$$ *Florida 1005; tel: (11) 4318-3000; fax: (11) 4318-3008; <www.marriottplaza. com.ar>.* Long the standard for glamour in the city, this hotel, right on Plaza San Martín and at the end of Calle Florida, opened in 1909. The architecture and decor are classic French. Some rooms have beautiful views of the Plaza. The Plaza Grill restaurant is the oldest in the city. 320 rooms.

Plaza San Martín Suites $$$ *Suipacha 1092; tel: (11) 4328-4740; fax: (11) 4328-9385.* This modern and efficient aparthotel is ideal for business people staying a number of days in Buenos Aires and who require comfort and excellent service. The Retiro location places guests just minutes from Plaza San Martín and the micro-center financial district. Rooms have kitchenettes. 54 rooms.

Sheraton Buenos Aires Hotel & Towers $$$$ *Calle San Martín 1225; tel: (11) 4318-9000; fax: (11) 4318-9353; <www. starwoodhotels.com>.* The city's largest hotel includes the Park Tower, an annex with 180 luxury rooms specially equipped for business travelers. Rooms in the main hotel are a bit institutional, though many have fine views of the Río de la Plata. El Aljibe is a good, formal restaurant; there's also a Japanese restaurant,

Tsuru. Separate pools for adults and kids, as well as spa, gym, and tennis courts. Wheelchair access. 742 rooms.

Sheraton Libertador Hotel $$$$ *Córdoba 690; tel: (11) 4321-0000; fax: (11) 4322-9703; <www.starwoodhotels.com>.* This handsome high-rise is one of the city's classic business hotels. The location in the microcenter unbeatable, and service impeccable, though some rooms are smarter than others. The expansive marble lobby is always humming with people. 194 rooms.

Recoleta

Alvear Palace Hotel $$$$ *Alvear 1891; tel: (11) 4808-2100; fax: (11) 4804-9246; <www.alvearpalace.com>.* The Alvear has been the classiest hotel in Buenos Aires since its inauguration in 1932. This French, Louis XVI-style building hosts stars and business magnates in all the luxury you can imagine, with prices to match. Its setting in Recoleta is refined and peaceful. Rooms are luxuriously Belle-Époque, but modern conveniences have been added. Its restaurant, La Bourgogne, is one of the city's finest. 200 rooms.

Caesar Park Hotel $$$$ *Posadas 1232; tel: (11) 4819-1100; fax: (11) 4819-1121; <www.caesar-park.com>.* In the midst of Recoleta, in front of the elegant Patio Bullrich shopping center, the slick, modern Caesar Park excels in services and facilities. Rooms and public areas are sumptuous, as are the bathrooms. Featuring several bars and 2 fine restaurants, this is one of the top choices for business travelers and one of the city's most expensive. Indoor pool. Wheelchair access. 170 rooms.

Etoile Hotel $$$$ *Pte. Roberto M. Ortiz 1835; tel: (11) 4805-2626; fax: (11) 4805-3613; <www.etoile.com.ar>.* This mid-sized hotel is ideally located if you want to experience the luxury of the surrounding *barrio*, Recoleta. Rooms are suites and have tantalizing views of the neighborhood; some rooms are much better than others, so ask to upgrade if you're not happy. It's a comfortable, relaxing place to stay with top-notch service. 96 rooms.

Hotel Plaza Francia $$$ *E. Schiaffino 2189; tel and fax: (11) 4804-9631; <www.hotelplazafrancia.com>*. This small hotel is tucked away on a street behind Plaza Francia. It's right in the middle of Recoleta, but with easy access to Avenida Libertador and either downtown or Palermo. Upper-floor front rooms have lovely views of the parks and gardens of Recoleta. 50 rooms.

Meliá Recoleta Plaza Hotel $$$ *Posadas 1557; tel: (11) 5353-4000; fax: (11) 5353-4001; <www.solmelia.com>*. This small hotel has a quiet Recoleta location for a reasonable price. The hotel's public rooms are attractive and European-styled. Rooms are plush, and many have marble bathrooms and separate sitting areas. 57 rooms.

Park Hyatt Buenos Aires $$$$ *Avenida Alvéar 1661; tel: (11) 5171-1234; fax: (11) 5171-1235, <www.buenosaires.park. hyatt.com>*. This luxury hotel was carefully designed to maintain the ambience and look of French-style mansions in Buenos Aires. In fact, the building is completely harmonious with the next-door Art Nouveau mansion that has been incorporated into the hotel – and which now houses ultra-luxe suites. The Park Hyatt seems to attract all visiting rock star royalty, a fact reflected by the prices. It's also popular with first-class business travelers. Outdoor pool. Wheelchair access. 165 rooms.

Park Plaza Kempinski Hotel $$$ *Parera 183; tel: (11) 6777-0200; fax: (11) 6777-0290; <www.parkplazahotels.com>*. This small European-styled hotel is a treat. Guests are received warmly, and the personal treatment continues throughout their stay. Floors have been named for great artists, and rooms are decorated with taste. The Park Plaza has a dedicated following of return guests. 54 rooms.

Wilton Palace Hotel $$$ *Callao 1162; tel/fax: (11) 4811-1818; <www.hotelwilton.com.ar>*. This mid-size hotel on the fringes of Recoleta and Barrio Norte is very good value. Rooms are fairly large and well-equipped. With its babysitting service and 24-hour business center, the hotel is popular with both families and business travelers. 120 rooms.

Recommended Restaurants

Buenos Aires is a fine city in which to eat out, as dining is one of *porteños'* favorite nighttime activities. Dining options run the gamut from simple, familiar places to sophisticated European-style restaurants, but most often dining in Argentina means meat. A steakhouse is called a *parrilla*, the feast of mixed grilled meats it serves that will put you under the table, a *parrillada*. Dining out in Buenos Aires is at present very reasonable, and one of the best deals available is the *menú ejecutivo*, a lunch-time, fixed-price meal consisting of 2, 3, or 4 courses. Restaurants generally display menus both outside and inside, so you can compare prices before committing. The restaurants listed in the following pages accept major credit cards unless otherwise stated.

$$$$	over US$15
$$$	US$10–15
$$	US$5–10
$	under US$5

San Telmo

La Brigada $$ *Estados Unidos 465; tel: (11) 4361-4685.* Open daily for lunch and dinner. Located in the fashionable and beautiful neighborhood of San Telmo, La Brigada offers a tasty *parrilla* and a good selection of Argentine wine. Its specialty is offal, which they claim is the best in Buenos Aires.

La Casa de Esteban de Luca $$ *Defensa 1000; tel: (11) 4361-4338.* Open Tuesday–Sunday for lunch and dinner. This colonial house was declared a National Historic Monument (it is the former home of the poet who wrote Argentina's national anthem). The menu is very homey and well-prepared. In addition to meat entrees, several good fish dishes, including grilled salmon and sole, are available, as is an excellent selection of Argentine wines. Very crowded on weekends.

Puerto Madero

Amma Café $ *Janana Manso 1652; tel: (11) 5787-1367.* Open daily for lunch and dinner. One of the many stylish eateries to pop up around Puerto Madero recently. Open every day this elegant café/deli serves fantastic fresh European-style sandwiches and salads.

Bahia Madero $$$ *Avenida Alicia Moreau de Justo 430; tel: (11) 4319-8733.* Open daily for lunch and dinner. A popular and accessible restaurant for young people, Bahia Madero frequently has live music. Like many inexpensive but chic restaurants, it focuses on pizza and pasta, but also has crêpes, shellfish, and an unusually impressive wine list.

Bice $$$ *Avenida Alicia Moreau de Justo 192; tel: (11) 4315-6216.* Open daily for lunch and dinner. A Northern Italian standard with locations in a handful of the world's most celebrated cities, including the original in Milan, this outlet has been around since 1994, when Puerto Madero was just beginning to shine. The décor is sedate but elegant; however, the dining room can be noisy. Risottos and pastas with interesting twists are the stars.

Cabaña Las Lilas $$$$ *Avenida Alicia Moreau de Justo 516; tel: (11) 4313-1336.* Open daily for lunch and dinner. This *parrilla* wins many votes as Buenos Aires's best restaurant for grilled meats. Extremely popular, it serves big beef – and it served a big beef eater in 1997, when President Clinton feasted here. Try the *ojo de bife* (ribeye steak). Las Lilas is a handsome place, with original artwork, brick walls, and windows overlooking the docks. It draws business people during lunch and chic couples at night.

Happening Puerto Madero $$$$ *Avenida Alicia Moreau de Justo 310; tel: (11) 4319-8712.* Open daily for lunch and dinner. This stylish restaurant, which has been in Puerto Madero since 1995, offers a wide variety of dishes, including excellent shellfish, but its specialty is meat. The cuts of meat are terrific, but if you're tiring of carnivorous pursuits, you can also have good fish and pasta.

El Mirasol $$$–$$$$ *Avenida Alicia Moreau de Justo 202; tel: (11) 4326-7322; <www.el-mirasol.com.ar>*. Open daily for lunch and dinner. A large and impressive *parrilla*, El Mirasol (The Sunflower) draws a sophisticated and stylish crowd. It offers excellent salads and *empanadas*. Dine on the outdoor verandah; tables have views of the beautiful people strolling the docks.

Montserrat & Center

Azurra $$$ *Corrientes 222, Microcentro; tel: (11) 4315-8381*. Open Monday–Friday for lunch and dinner; Saturday dinner only. A great place to sample modern Argentine cuisine whilst gazing at the fantastic views it offers of the city. The service is excellent, and the decor and ambiance very inviting.

La Estancia $$$ *Lavalle 941; tel: (11) 4326-0330*. Open daily for lunch and dinner. La Estancia is one of Buenos Aires's classic *parrillas*. The grilled beef and kid goat are terrific, and it's one of the most attractively priced of the city's steakhouses. It draws many business people from the surrounding area.

Catalinas $$$$ *Reconquista 875; tel: (11) 4313-0182*. Open Monday–Friday for lunch and dinner; weekends dinner only. This French restaurant has attractive country-style décor and an inventive menu. The seafood and game are wonderfully prepared by chef Ramiro Pardo and his team. Catalinas is very elegant and expensive, but a more economical way to enjoy the food and ambience here is to take advantage of one of the prix-fixe menus that are designed according to season. Desserts are outstanding.

Clásica y Moderna $$ *Callao 892; tel: (11) 4812-8707*. Open daily for lunch and dinner (open late). A handsome café/bar/restaurant and bookstore, it also features live music – jazz and tango. The menu is basic but varied, serving salads, tortillas, chicken and fish. A high-value midday hot and cold *tenedor libre* (all-you-can-eat offer), including a glass of wine, is a real bargain.

Dorá $$$ *L.N. Alem 1016; tel: (11) 4311-2891.* Open Monday–Saturday for lunch and dinner. Dora has long-time clients who insist that it's the best in the city. If you have old friends in the city – the kind who want to impress you with honest cooking rather than flashy surroundings – they may bring you here. Thick, juicy steaks and seafood are equally excellent, and portions are large.

Los Inmortales $$ *Paraná 1209; tel: (11) 4311-2222.* Open daily for lunch and dinner. This is no mere pizzeria; it's become an institution. Fans say it serves the perfect Argentine pizza, but the homemade pastas are also popular. The restaurant is simple but attractive. *Empanadas* make an excellent appetizer. The 'immortals' refered to in the name are Carlos Gardel and other Argentine stars. Other branches at Lavalle 746, Callao 1165, M. T. de Alvear 1256, and Junín 1727.

Tomo I $$$$ *Carlos Pelligrini 525 (in Hotel Crowne Plaza Panamericano); tel: (11) 4326-6695.* Open Tuesday–Sunday for lunch and dinner; Monday dinner only. One of the most bally-hooed restaurants in the whole city is found in a large, 5-star hotel right on 9 de Julio. The kitchen produces innovative Italian and French dishes in an elegant setting. The combinations of unusual tastes are always surprising. The restaurant is a favorite of theater- and opera-goers.

Retiro & Barrio Norte

Broccolino $$ *Esmeralda 776; tel: (11) 4322-7754.* Open daily for lunch and dinner. A relaxed and inviting Italian tratto-ria, this busy, noisy, family-run place is crowded with both locals and visitors to the city. A great oven produces pizzas and foccacia, and there are mouth-watering pastas, of course. No credit cards.

Filo $$ *San Martín 975; tel: (11) 4311-0312.* Open for lunch and dinner (open late). A hip and colorful restaurant that looks more like a *boliche,* the menu is mostly fancy pizzas and pastas. There's a massive circular pizza oven toward the back, where a pizza dough kneader works diligently. The crowd is young, stylish, and energetic.

Morizono $$$$ *Reconquista 899; tel: (11) 4314-0924.* Open for lunch and dinner. Sushi has caught on in Buenos Aires as it has elsewhere, and many feel that this is the best sushi and Japanese food in the city. The food is fresh and wonderful, and the restaurant, which has two levels, is stylish.

Las Nazarenas $$$ *Reconquista 1132; tel: (11) 4312-5559.* Open daily for lunch and dinner. This *asador criollo* is a classic porteño barbecue house. Directly across from the giant Sheraton hotel, you can't miss the attention-getting façade of this colonial building sandwiched between tall office buildings. The cozy and bustling two-story *parrilla* has a long and varied menu, but all anyone seems to eat is Angus beef. The *bife de chorizo* is especially good. A fine wine list is all-Argentine. A day and night *menú especial* is a bargain.

El Sanjuanino $ *Posadas 1515; tel: (11) 4804-2909.* Open for lunch and early dinner. The specialty at this simple neighborhood restaurant is the *empanada,* the classic Argentine turnover, most often served as an appetizer. The *empanadas* are wonderful here, and you can easily make a whole meal from them. The sangría also has many fans. No credit cards.

Recoleta

Au Bec Fin $$$$ *Vicente López 1827; tel: (11) 4807-3765.* Open Tuesday–Sunday for dinner. Expect excellent French cooking and impressive service at this sophisticated Recoleta restaurant, which has earned its place at the top of Buenos Aires's food chain. The decor is opulent, and private upstairs salons are perfect for private dinners. The menu is creative, and the wine list suitably outstanding.

La Bourgogne $$$$ *2027 Ayacucho (in Alvear Palace Hotel); tel: (11) 4805-3897.* Open daily for lunch and dinner. La Bourgogne is reputed to be the best restaurant in Buenos Aires, if not in the entire country. Meticulously prepared and innovative French food in elegant surroundings is the secret here. Argentines say it's a place to go at least once in your life. Excellent wine list.

Cumaná $ *Rodriguez Peña 1149; tel: (11) 4813-9207.* Open daily for lunch and dinner. This lively place serves traditional snacks at very reasonable prices. It is known for its *empanadas*, cooked in a traditional adobe oven, typical of Northern Argentina.

Sottovoce $$ *Libertador 1098; tel: (11) 4807-6691.* Open daily for lunch and dinner. This restaurant, with its warm wooden interior, serves simple yet delicious Italian cuisine. Try the homemade pasta, a favorite with the locals.

Palermo

A Los Amigos $$ *Loyola 701; tel: (11) 4777-0422.* Open daily for lunch and dinner. This very familiar, 50-year-old restaurant is highly valued by its regular customers. It serves excellent home-cooking, including 'grandma's omelets,' homemade pastas, and grilled steaks. The walls are lined with old photos of boxing and *fútbol* champions. No credit cards.

Anastasia $$$$ *Bulnes 2593, corner of Cabello; tel: (11) 4802-8640/4808-0499.* Open daily for lunch and dinner. A slick and elegant *parrilla* option in Palermo. Offers fantastic cuts of meat and a great wine list. As the service is excellent and the portions enormous, you are unlikely to leave dissatisfied.

Angelín $$ *Avenida Córdoba 5270, between Godoy Cruz and Uriarte; tel: (11) 4776-4100.* Open daily for dinner. Among locals this place has the reputation of being the best pizza joint in the city. Although small in size, and a little rough round the edges, the pizza is delicious. Situated in the heart of Palermo Viejo it is a great place to hang with the locals. Try the popular and delicious *pizza fugazza* (cheese and onion topped pizza).

Casa Cruz $$$ *Uriarte 1658; tel: (11) 4833-1112.* Open Monday–Saturday from 8.30pm. One of the newer high-profile restaurants in Palermo. Casa Cruz has an elegant ambiance and the menu is as mouth watering as it is innovative.

Massey $$$$ *Arce 305; tel: (11) 4777-4216.* Open for dinner. This elegant Japanese restaurant is located in a chic dining area near Palermo Viejo. The chef is one of the most renowned in the city, and his restaurant one of Buenos Aires's most fashionable.

La Ochava $$$ *Baez 401 y Chenaut; tel: (11) 4776-3122.* Open daily for lunch and dinner. This comfortable, simple corner restaurant serves à la carte grilled meats, including chicken and salmon, as well as pastas and salads. The midday *menú ejecutivo* is an excellent, filling deal.

Ølsen $$ *Gorriti 5870, Palermo Hollywood; tel: (11) 4776-7677.* Open Tuesday–Saturday for lunch and dinner; Sunday breakfast, lunch and dinner; closed Monday. Another very popular recent addition to the trendy area of Palermo. Stunning decor accompanies an adventurous menu. Many Scandinavian delights are on offer here, cooked to perfection. There is also a large selection of vodkas and schnapps to savor.

Beyond Palermo

Aquellos Años $$$ *Avenida Rafael Obligado, Costanera Norte; tel: (11) 4784-8681.* Families have been coming for years to gorge on first-rate *parrilla* in simple surroundings. It's a big, busy, and noisy place on the riverfront. Take as large an appetite as you can, as you'll be served embarrassing quantities of beef, salad, and fries. The *bife de chorizo* wins many accolades.

Contigó Peru $ *Echeverría 1627 y Montañeses, Belgrano; tel: (11) 4780-3960.* Open Tuesday–Sunday for lunch and dinner. Situated in the residential area of Belgrano, northwest of Palermo, this is a laid-back place popular with Peruvians living in Buenos Aires. The food here is good – those new to Peruvian cuisine may be surprised by its similarities with Chinese food.

INDEX